Kaleidoscope

3 Reading and Writing

Anita Sökmen
University of Washington

Daphne Mackey
University of Washington

HOUGHTON MIFFLIN COMPANY   Boston   New York

Director of ESL Programs: Susan Maguire
Senior Associate Editor: Kathleen Sands Boehmer
Associate Project Editor: Gabrielle Stone
Senior Production/Design Coordinator: Carol Merrigan
Manufacturing Manager: Florence Cadran
Marketing Manager: Elaine Leary
Freelance Developmental Editor: Kathleen M. Smith

Cover Design: Ha Nguyen
Cover Image: Tony Craddock. Tony Stone Images.

www.hmco.com/college

Printed in the U.S.A.

Library of Congress Catalog Card Number: 98-72235

ISBN: 0-395-85882-8

456789-QF-09 08 07 06 05

To Suheyl and Joseph, and George and Caroline.

Acknowledgments

We would like to thank our families for their support and understanding as we turned our focus to our computers. We are grateful for the feedback of colleagues and students at the University of Washington.

In particular, we thank Cara Izumi, Eleanor Holstein, Lesley Lin, Mi-Ran Park, Suranto, Jane Power, Mary Kay Seales, Jim Ward, and Nancy Ackles, for her knowledge of article use. We also appreciated the comments of reviewers: Brad Beachy, Butler Community College, KS; Mary Stehley, Rice University, TX; Betty Volpe, Norwalk Community College, CT; Norman Prange, Cuyahoga Community College, OH; Beverly Beisbier, San Jose Community College, CA; Christine Uber Gross, Thunderbird, Amer. Graduate School of International Business, AZ; Jackie George, Seattle Central Community College, WA; Kim Benson, American Language Institute, CA; and Dean Dugan, Mercy College, NY.

Thanks also to the people at Houghton Mifflin who have been so great to work with: Susan Maguire, Kathy Sands-Boehmer, Kathy Smith, and Gabrielle Stone.

Contents

Unit 6   Beyond Your Limits   *195*

16   Risk Takers   *196*

17   First Aid on the Mountain   *204*

18   Playing Hard   *219*

Preface

Kaleidoscope 3: Reading and Writing provides intermediate students with a variety of tasks designed to improve reading and writing skills. It is based on the premises that students

- need more than humanities-based types of writing experiences.
- need to develop a working vocabulary within a variety of topics.
- need to learn how to edit their own work.

Overview

Kaleidoscope 3 introduces students to the fundamentals of academic, business, technical, and practical everyday writing. *Kaleidoscope 3*

- integrates reading and writing skills.
- focuses on vocabulary development, a key skill in both reading and writing.
- works on key reading skills that help prepare students to deal with authentic texts.
- recycles skills in a variety of ways.
- focuses on multigenre writing.
- includes **Preparing to Write** and **Editing and Rewriting** criteria that help less-experienced instructors feel comfortable with different types of writing assignments.
- uses task-based exercises as much as possible to keep students involved and to reduce the amount of wordiness in the text.
- allows each student to stay within his or her comfort level for sharing information and experiences.
- includes ideas for class activities.
- includes a **Reference** section with helpful information such as spelling rules, irregular verb forms, rules for using and forming comparatives and superlatives, and formats for formal business letters.

Features

With some variation, the chapters include these main elements and follow this general format:

Starting Point   Connects students to the topic of the chapter.

Reading	Includes exercises that focus on comprehension, skill-building, and vocabulary.
Targeting	Helps students work with vocabulary and key expressions related to a topic or a type of writing.
Writing	Includes **Preparing to Write** activities that help students develop ideas and write in a variety of formats. The length of compositions has been left open to fit the curricula of various programs.
Editing and Rewriting	Teaches students how to edit their own writing with a focus on the most common mistakes in writing and suggestions for what students ought to look for as they check their work. The **Editing Checklist** includes questions for students to use in editing their peers' writing and their own writing.

Additional activities in *Kaleidoscope 3* include **Quickwriting** and suggestions for a **Class Activity** to round out many of the topics. Depending on whether the writing and editing activities are done during class, each chapter will take from one to three hours of class time. For longer, more extensive reading assignments on the topics, instructors can supplement the readings with additional authentic materials or have students find readings on their own. Good sources for student searches include the Internet, newspapers, magazines, or the library. It is also possible to recycle kinds of writing assignments from later units if more writing practice is needed. Exercises that have answers in the back of the book are marked with the (ANSWER KEY) icon.

Becoming self-editors can be an overwhelming task for ESL students. We therefore suggest training students to do multiple passes through their compositions, focusing on one type of error at a time. They will have a better chance of finding errors this way than if they are trying to find all types of mistakes in one pass. For this reason, editing exercises focus on one type of error at a time. As each type has been covered in class, encourage students to build up a routine of multiple passes through their work in the editing stage. For example,

- one pass through to look for sentence completeness.
- one pass to focus on verb tenses.
- another pass to look at nouns: do they need an article? do they need to be plural?

As the term progresses, your feedback on writing will help students know what type of error they should pay most attention to.

Student Notebook

We suggest that students use a reading/writing notebook. Possible uses for the notebook include

- quickwriting as indicated in the text.
- journal writing if teachers find this activity beneficial.
- keeping track of outside reading with a reading "log" and brief notes about readings: new vocabulary, questions, and interesting ideas.
- reflecting on their progress as writers—what have they learned after completing their work in a topic.

Vocabulary Strategies

In order for students to learn the new vocabulary that they record in their notebooks, they need to use it. Here are some suggestions for helping students practice the vocabulary.

- Have students look in newspapers or magazines for vocabulary that they have studied in *Kaleidoscope 3*. Have them write the sentences they find and share them with the class.
- Have students find words in their notebooks from different chapters that could be used in a conversation. Have them write that conversation.
- Ask them to find five adjectives from their notebooks and, working in small groups, determine the opposites. Have them make a matching exercise to give to other groups.
- Suggest that students look through the vocabulary in their notebooks for words that are related in meaning. They can then make up related word lists with one word that doesn't fit. Then have them write sentences or paragraphs using some of the related words.
- Ask students to choose phrasal verbs (verbs with prepositions) or collocations (groups of words that go together) from the

vocabulary in their notebooks. Have them write sentences with these expressions, leaving a blank for one of the words in the expression. They can then take turns quizzing the other students on the missing words.

- Have students make flash cards by writing words and short definitions on opposite sides of index cards to practice with or use in a game.
- Create a vocabulary search game by giving students a certain amount of time to find words in their notebooks related to work, exercise, family, and other topics.
- Have students list nouns from their notebooks and use dictionaries to find the other forms in that word family. Students can teach these forms to the class.
- Ask students to find words that have the same suffix, prefix, or root. Have them compile the results in a table.
- Have students make drawings to represent words from their notebooks and ask their classmates to guess the words.
- Have students work in groups to make a crossword puzzle of words from their notebooks. Then they can exchange their puzzles with classmates.
- In a game of word clues, have students choose words from their notebooks and write them on slips of paper. Working in pairs, each student chooses a word and gives clues about it to his or her partner, who tries to guess the word. After five minutes, have them change roles or switch partners.
- In group brainstorming, have students think of synonyms for words from their notebooks. They may use a dictionary. Have them make a scrambled list of the synonyms and use them for a matching quiz. Do the same for antonyms.
- Have students choose five words from their notebooks and survey native speakers for the first word that comes to mind when they hear the target word. Ask them to share the word association results with the rest of the class.

Kaleidoscope 3 AT A GLANCE*

Unit	Reading	Preparing to Write	Writing	Targeting Language	Editing and Rewriting
1 What's In a Name?	• scanning (1) • analyzing vocabulary (1) (3) • inferences (2) • taking notes in a chart (2) • analyzing reference (2) • applying information (3) • main idea & specific information(3) • skimming (3)	• analyzing style and format (1) • collecting ideas (3) • providing supporting ideas (3)	• writing a letter, fax, or e-mail message (1) • description of your name (3)	• collocations for describing names (3)	• sentence completeness (1) • verb tense errors (3)
2 Food for Thought	• inferences (4) • context (4, 6) • applying information (4) • identifying specific and general information (4) • taking notes in a chart or diagram (4, 5) • analyzing word forms (4) • identifying topics (5)(6) • predicting (6) • skimming (6)	• designing a chart (4) • brainstorming (clustering ideas) (5) • supporting details (6)	• writing a chart (4) • customs (5) • review (6)	• ways to give advice (5) • expressions for reviews and recommendations (6)	• consistency in charts and lists (4) • gerunds and infinitives (5) • punctuation problems: colons and semicolons (6)
3 Musical Notes	• scanning (7) • analyzing reference (7) • taking notes in a chart or timeline (7, 9) • analyzing support (7) • summarizing (7, 9) • analyzing vocabulary (8) • prediction (8, 9) • identifying topic (9)	• Using a timeline (7) • Analyzing parts of definitions (8) • Mapping in a diagram (9) • Organizing support (9)	• personal narrative (7) • technical definitions (8) • description (9)	• word forms (7) • transitions (9)	• adjective clause/ of/ for phrase errors (8) • punctuation with subordinating conjunctions and adverbial expressions (9)

*The numbers in parentheses refer to chapters.

1 What's in a Name?

In this first unit, you will read and write about different customs for naming children and changing names.

These are some of the activities you will do in this unit:

- Read about confusion over names
- Write a business communication about a name problem
- Read about naming issues and customs
- Read a description of a name
- Write a description of your name

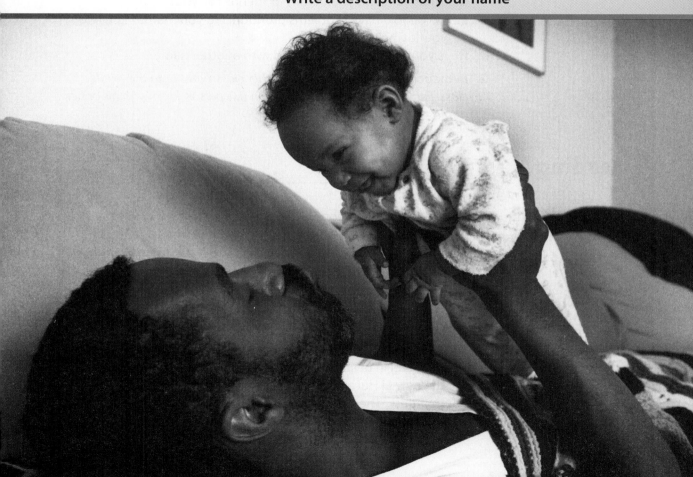

Chapter 1

Hello, My Name Is . . .

It's easy to make a mistake in spelling or pronouncing people's names. In this chapter you will read about mistakes with names and write formal and informal communications to clear up name confusion.

Starting Point

Introductions

Although every person is an individual, most names are not unique.

1. *Discuss these questions with a classmate:*

   a. What's your name?
   b. Does your name have a meaning?
   c. What name would you like to be called in class?
   d. What name do your family or friends call you?
   e. Do people have problems pronouncing your name? Spelling your name?
   f. Is your name often confused with another name?

2. *Introduce your classmate to two other classmates or to the whole class. Explain any common confusion this person faces with his or her name.*

Reading

Name-Starved China

Have you ever met someone with the same first and last name as yours? Imagine knowing several people with the same names! This reading tells what can happen when a culture has a limited number of last names available.

1. *Read the following selection.*

Name-Starved China

[1] Li Hui's identity crisis hit rock bottom when he started working at the Grand Hotel in Beijing a few years ago. He quickly discovered he wasn't the only Li Hui around. In fact, he wasn't even the only Li Hui at the front desk. There were two, including him, while a third worked in the financial department. When another pair of Li Huis showed up

for training months later, phone messages were a headache and office contests were a nightmare ("And the winner is: Li Hui!").

[2] Eventually, Li, 28, escaped the hotel business—but not his identity crisis. Now he listens to radio personality Li Hui read the morning headlines. Two of his buddies have other friends called Li Hui. By his own reckoning, Li has met six people in Beijing alone who have his name. He knows of many more. "Maybe I'll form a Li Hui club!" he joked one afternoon.

[3] China has one-fifth of the world's population but a much smaller fraction of its surnames. Of the 12,000 surnames that existed in China centuries ago, 3,100 remain today. This is a tiny number for 1.2 billion people. Indeed, the nation's top five family names (Li, Wang, Zhang, Liu, Chen) cover nearly one-third of the population, or 350 million citizens. That would be the same as everyone in the United States and Mexico sharing just five last names. There are 87 million Chinese with the surname of Li. In comparison, only 2.4 million Americans are named Smith, the most widespread surname in the English-speaking world.

[4] If you combine the shrinking surname supply with a serious lack of invention by many parents, you wind up with thousands of Chinese who have the same names. Along with this are numerous instances of mistaken identity. Lab tests get mixed up, as in the case of the man who told relatives he had inoperable cancer. Fortunately for this man, the unlucky patient turned out to be someone else. Love letters get opened by the wrong blushing recipients. There are even cases of suspects getting arrested for crimes they did not commit. One man was mistakenly arrested in Shandong province because his name matched the criminal's. It also matched the local security chief's!

[5] The confusion is enough to cause some of China's scholars to warn of serious problems ahead if there isn't more name variety. However, that's not easy in a culture where names are very important. Many believe names determine a person's destiny. Parents are reluctant to choose uncommon names. Because they are afraid of causing bad luck for their offspring, many pay for a name master to give their child a name that will bring good fortune.

2. *Practice **scanning** quickly for specific information. Scan the reading and find the answers to these questions:*

   a. What hotel did Li Hui work at? _____

   b. How old is Li Hui? _____

   c. What city does Li Hui live in? _____

   d. How many surnames are there in China today? _____

   e. What are the five most popular surnames? _____
_____

   f. How many people have the family name of Li in China? _____
_____

   g. What is the most common family name in the United States?
_____

   h. What are three examples of mistaken identity? _____
_____

3. *Look at the selection again. **Analyze the vocabulary** in the context of the reading to determine the meaning of these words. Use the context and your own knowledge to help you decide which choice is the best. Put a check next to your answer. The first one has been done for you.*

   a. In an *identity crisis*, a person is

      ✓ having a hard time figuring out who he or she is.
      _____ facing an emergency.

   b. When you hit *rock bottom*, you

      _____ are at a very low point.
      _____ are having an accident.

   c. *By his own reckoning* means

      _____ "by his own counting."
      _____ "in his area."

   d. *Shrinking surnames* means that

      _____ the family names are getting shorter.
      _____ the supply of family names is decreasing.

e. A *fraction* means
    _____ a small part of something.
    _____ a large part of something.

f. A *lack of invention* on the part of parents has resulted in
    _____ not selecting unusual names.
    _____ being creative about name choices.

g. A person's *destiny* is
    _____ what a person chooses to do in life.
    _____ what a person is meant to do with his or her life.

h. When choosing a name, parents are *reluctant* to deviate from the tried and true. This means they are
    _____ willing to try new names.
    _____ not willing to try new names.

Reflect on Reading

In exercise 2, you **scanned** the reading to look for specific information. Sometimes certain words and numbers are easy to find because they look different from other information. Match the following information with the descriptions. You may need to use some choices more than once.

Explanations	_d_	**a.** usually have numbers
Names	_____	**b.** usually have numbers or names of months
Lists	_____	**c.** usually have capital letters
Dates	_____	**d.** may be in parentheses ( )
Ages	_____	**e.** may have commas separating them

Writing

Preparing to Write: Analyzing the Style and Format

Nowadays, people use a lot of different formats to communicate with each other. This section presents examples of a formal letter, a fax, and e-mail (electronic mail) messages.

1. *Read the formal letter, fax, and e-mail messages on pages 6 and 7.*

Enrique Guzman Salamonca
45 Highland Terrace
Denver, Colorado 80203

June 1, 1998

Maureen Stutzman
International Student Office
Norfolk Community College
60 Center Street
Alexandria, VA 22314

Dear Ms. Stutzman:

The enclosed I-20 form lists my last name as Salamonca. In Colombia, where I am from, people use their father's surname followed by their mother's surname when they state their whole name. When only one surname is used, it should be the father's.

Please send me a new form using the surname Guzman. Thank you for making this change.

Sincerely,

Enrique Guzman Salamonca

Enrique Guzman Salamonca

FAX

TO: Maureen Stutzman
International Student Office

FAX: 703-475-3840

FROM: Ana Valovis *A. V.*

DATE: September 21, 1998

Message:

Yesterday I received the supporting documents that I need to apply for my visa. Unfortunately, there is a spelling mistake, and the name on the documents does not match the name on my passport.

Please correct this mistake and send me new documents as soon as possible. I need to submit the application by the end of the week.

Thank you very much.

Date: Tues, 14 Jul 9:25:33 -0700 (PDT)
From: "Maureen Stutzman" <mstutz@norfolkcc.edu>
To: Hilary Thorpe <hilaryt@norfolkcc.edu>
Subject: Schedule

Sorry Hilary! We have a Hillary (2 l's) in our office. I'll have to be more careful with my spelling. I typed Hilary and our e-mail system addressed it to you automatically.

Maureen

Forwarded message

Date: Mon, 13 Jul 1998 15:16:58 -0700 (PDT)
From: Hilary Thorpe <hilaryt@norfolkcc.edu>
To: "Maureen Stutzman" <mstutz@norfolkcc.edu>
Subject: Schedule

Hi,

I'm not sure why you sent me this message. Please give me some more information if you need me to do anything.

Hilary

Forwarded message

Date: Mon, 13 Jul 1998 10:12:03 -0700 (PDT)
From: "Maureen Stutzman" <mstutz@norfolkcc.edu>
To: Hilary Thorpe <hilaryt@norfolkcc.edu>
Subject: Schedule

Hilary,

Please check to see if the changes have been made in the copy of the schedule. If they have, then you can print it and put it in the folders.

Thanks,

Maureen

ANSWER KEY

2. *Answer the following questions about the letter, fax, and e-mail messages.*

　　a. List the problems related to names in the letter, fax, and e-mail messages.

　　　letter: _____

　　　fax: _____

　　　e-mail messages: _____

　　b. Analyze the style and format in the letter, fax, and e-mail messages. Put a check to indicate which feature each one has.

	Letter	Fax	E-mail
name and address of sender			
name and address of receiver			
date			
salutation with a colon (:)			
a sentence or two of greeting			
the main message in the first couple of sentences			
a closing			
formal use of language			
informal use of language			
incomplete sentences			
indenting the first line of a paragraph			
single spacing in paragraphs			
double spacing between paragraphs			

c. What makes the letter and fax more formal than the e-mail messages? Find specific examples to show this difference.

_____

_____

d. How about differences in tone? Do any of the writers seem friendlier than others? Explain. _____

_____

e. The fax in exercise 1 contains a message. When you send faxes, you can put the message in this format or you can send a fax "cover sheet" and put the message in a formal letter. On separate paper, change the fax to a fax cover sheet and a formal letter to Maureen Stutzman.

Writing a Letter, a Fax, or an E-mail Message

Think of a problem that could happen related to your name or someone else's name. Write about this problem in **two** formats, a formal letter and either a fax or an e-mail message.

> A formal letter follows business letter format.
>
> For examples of business letter format, see pages 237–238 in Reference.

Editing and Rewriting

Editing for Sentence Completeness

Sometimes it is difficult to decide if a sentence is complete or not.

1. _Study the following facts about sentences._

Rules	Incorrect Examples	Correct Examples
A complete sentence has a subject and a verb.	This unusual name.	This **is** an unusual name.
Words like "that," "who," and "because" can connect two ideas that have their own subject and verb.	**Because** my parents wanted me to have success in life. (This is an incomplete sentence because it has only one idea, and you need another main idea with "because.") The name **that I was given.** (The main idea is missing.)	I was given a very strong name because my parents wanted me to have success in life. OR Because my parents wanted me to have success in life, I was given a very strong name. The name that I was given is a traditional woman's name.
Two complete sentences cannot be connected by a comma. Separate them into two sentences or connect them with a conjunction, a transition word, or a semicolon.	My dad wanted to call me Sugar because our last name was Cane, my mom hated that idea.	My dad wanted to call me Sugar because our last name was Cane. My mom hated that idea. My dad wanted to call me Sugar because our last name was Cane, **but** my mom hated that idea. **Although** my dad wanted to call me Sugar because our last name was Cane, my mom hated that idea. My dad wanted to call me Sugar because our last name was Cane; my mom hated that idea.

2. *Correct the errors in sentence completeness where necessary.*

(ANSWER KEY)

  a. The traditions and customs for naming different around the world.

  b. When I first came to America, using the titles of Mr. and Mrs. with a last name was a new concept for me. Because women in my country keep their family's surname after marriage.

  c. Some people insist that changing surnames damages women's identities, others think names do not influence identity.

  d. I think women all over the world should not change their surnames, keeping them has much more meaning to all women.

  e. It means men and women equal. Some people think that nontraditional approaches to surnames cause too much confusion. But I think this opinion is the result of being used to tradition.

  f. Though I live in a country where women keep their family names. I have never heard that it causes social confusion. Because the family doesn't necessarily mean the group of people who have the same surname.

Editing Checklist

Check the Content

1. *Exchange your letter and fax or e-mail message with a classmate. After you read your classmate's work, answer these questions:*

   ❏ Has the name problem been clearly explained?
   ❏ Is the language appropriate for the type of communication?

Check the Details

2. *Read your own writing again. If necessary, revise. Add or change details. Then continue checking your paper. Use these questions:*

   ❏ Did you include an address that is appropriate for each kind of communication?
   ❏ Is the form correct for each kind of communication?
   ❏ Is the tone appropriate for each?
   ❏ Are your sentences complete?

3. *Revise your writing.*

Vocabulary Log

What words or phrases would you like to remember from this chapter? Write five to ten items in your notebook. Be sure to include words that go with these items (prepositions, for example) and other forms of the word that you know. Also write a sentence so that you will remember how to use the new words. Here is an example.

confusion (n – noncount)

There was a lot of confusion when the names were called.

BE confused with (something else) (v)

BE confused about (something) (v)

My name, Brenner, is often confused with Brunner.

I am confused about what to call him: his first name or Mr. Kim?

CAUSE confusion
My last name often causes confusion because it is spelled differently than the usual spelling. I always have to spell it when I leave a message on the phone.

How can you learn the words that you list? Is there anything else that you would like to add to the information in your notebook? Discuss with a classmate and/or your instructor.

Grammar and Punctuation Review

Go back and read your writing in this chapter. What grammar and punctuation problems did you have? Write your errors and the corrected sentences in your notebook. Then use the correct grammar or punctuation again in new sentences. Review them before the next writing assignment.

Chapter 2

Identity Crisis

This chapter focuses on how decisions about naming can affect a person's identity.

Starting Point

Marriage Naming Customs

1. *In your culture do women change their surnames when they get married? Does this decision depend on level of education, religion, or region? Discuss these questions with a classmate.*

2. *Complete this table with statistics from the class. How many women in the class will change their last name when they marry (or have done so already)? How many will keep their family name? How many will add their husband's name to theirs? What would men in the class prefer that their wives do?*

	Women	*Men*
Woman changes surname to husband's surname		
Woman keeps her family name		
Woman adds husband's name to her family name		
Other *(Explain)*		

Reading

Breaking with Tradition

Life has changed a great deal for women in recent years, and so have customs regarding their last names.

Breaking with Tradition

It used to be a non-issue. When Jane Doe married Joe Snow, she became Jane Snow. But as gender roles change, more couples are breaking with tradition. These days, a married woman might remain Jane Doe or become Jane Doe Snow, or Jane Doe-Snow. Her husband might change his name, too, becoming Joe Snow-Doe, Joe Doe-Snow—or even Joe Doe. Some couples are choosing to merge their last names, becoming Jane and Joe Snowdoe.

"There's been all kinds of engineering with names," says Rae Moses, a linguistics professor at Northwestern University. Moses surveyed an Illinois grade school with 302 students and found that 32% of them—most of whose mothers were working professionals—had non-traditional last names.

As more options become acceptable, many couples are asking themselves: What's in a name? There's no shortage of answers. To some, the traditional method is a sexist vestige of the days when a woman literally became her husband's property. "It's a subtle but pervasive message that's passed along—that the line of heritage is male, that it's most important," says Sharon Dwyer, a Virginia Tech doctoral student who is researching the topic for her dissertation. To others, the tradition has long since shed that stigma and has become a romantic symbol of the bond between two people. To still others, it's a convenient way to dump an unwieldy name.

"I don't think it's ever going to be the norm, but I think we're going to see more of it in the future," says Scheuble. She has conducted studies on the subject with her husband, David Johnson, a sociologist at the University of Nebraska. "A strong majority of men and women said if a woman wants to keep her birth name, that's fine with them," Johnson says. But, Scheuble adds, people with

more education and higher income are more likely to be tolerant of a woman keeping her name, as are people who grew up in large cities. Political and religious leanings also seemed to affect attitudes.

Hillary Rodham Clinton went up against those attitudes in Arkansas. When Bill Clinton was first elected governor in 1978, Hillary used the last name Rodham. But after Bill lost the 1980 election, she became Hillary Clinton to appeal to socially conservative voters. Bill Clinton won reelection in 1982. To this day, however, some people resent her use of Rodham as a middle name.

Randee Schuster Motzkin of Santa Monica didn't have political concerns, but she, too, waited a while after marriage to add her husband's last name. "At first I had no connection to this Randee Motzkin person," recalls the 28 year-old attorney. "I felt connected to my family. It's hard to undo what you've done for 26 years. You have to ease into this new identity of spouse." After about a year, she officially became a Motzkin. "It creates this cement link between husband and wife," she says.

Other couples have come up with different ways to create that bond. When Jeff Nicholson of Champaign, Ill., married Dawn Owens, he became Nicholson-Owens, she became Owens-Nicholson. "I felt it would make me feel a lot closer to her," says Jeff, 24. "And it seemed fairest. Neither of us loses our heritage in the family tree." Dawn, 31, says her family wasn't thrilled when she broke the news. "My mom was really looking forward to saying, 'Mr. and Mrs. Jeffrey Nicholson.'" So, apparently, was the Illinois Department of Motor Vehicles. "We had to fight them tooth and nail to get a hyphen on our driver's license," Dawn says. "They said their software wouldn't take it."

Logistical hassles aren't uncommon for couples who buck tradition. In some cases, society just isn't set up for

husband and wife to have different names. Couples often have difficulties with mortgage applications, bank credit cards, and other financial records.

In St. Louis, Joseph Keel, formerly Joseph Bubeck, says he encountered reverse discrimination when he took his wife's last name. His credit card company refused to change his name over the phone, even though they said they would do it for a woman. "I got sort of irate," says Keel, 34, a medical student. When he suggested to a supervisor that the policy might be discriminatory, he got his way. Keel says he wasn't trying to make a feminist statement when he took his wife's name. The couple wanted the same last name, and Joseph just liked Keel better than Bubeck.

Pete Schult of Santa Cruz took his wife's name for the same reason. He figured Schult sounded a lot better than Dombrowsky. Julia, 30, was relieved she didn't have to become a Dombrowsky.

Nancy Herman of Minneapolis and her husband, Don Perlmutter, came up with yet another variation: They merged their names, becoming the Perlmans.

Several other countries do have different naming methods. "Around the world, it's not seen as a big deal if a woman keeps her name," says Dwyer, the doctoral student. In some Scandinavian and Latin American countries, married women often keep their names. In Japan, says Northwestern's Moses, if a woman with no siblings marries into a family that has several sons, her husband will sometimes take her family name. "It's kind of a gift that the groom's family gives to the bride's family," Moses says.

Cathie Whittenburg of Portland, Me., was determined that her last name would be passed down. Her daughter, born first, has the last name of her husband, Lenny Shedletsky. But her son is a Whittenburg. As for what names the grandkids will get, Lenny says his children will have to figure that one out on their own.

2. An **inference** is something you understand from a reading, but the writer doesn't state directly. Use inference to decide which of the following statements are true. Circle the letter of each statement that is true. Be prepared to defend your answers.

   a. It's a tradition for women to keep their surnames when they marry.

   b. Men are expected to keep their surnames when they marry.

   c. Scheuble and Johnson's studies show that most unmarried women plan to change their last name when they marry.

   d. Most people in the U.S. are tolerant of women keeping their birth names.

   e. If a woman changes her name to her husband's last name, she is expressing a deeply held belief.

   f. When couples in the U.S. have different last names, it can cause confusion for government agencies and businesses.

   g. In the U.S. it is legal for a woman to keep her birth name or hyphenate her name with her husband's, but it is not legal to take a name that is different from hers or her husband's.

   h. Swedish married women usually keep their birth names.

   i. Children in families with unusual last names use traditional naming patterns when they grow up and have children.

Reflect on Reading

In exercise 2, you had to **infer** meaning. When you compared your answers with your classmates' answers, you probably found that you didn't always agree. There may have been more than one correct answer. **Inferences** are often not clear-cut because they are not stated directly in the reading.

3. **Taking notes in a chart** will help you understand information in a reading. Complete this chart with information about different ways to deal with the surname problem when couples get married.

Type	Description	Example from the Reading
traditional	*woman takes husband's last name*	Jane Dow → Jane Snow when she marries Joe Snow
nontraditional	woman keeps birth name	_____ _____
	_____	Nancy Herman and Don Perlmutter → the Perlmans
	woman keeps birth surname as middle name	_____ _____
	couple hyphenates name	_____ _____
	_____	Joseph Bubeck → Joseph Keel

4. *Writers often use pronouns or demonstrative adjectives to **refer** to nouns mentioned before. What do the underlined words in each item refer to? Look in the reading. The paragraph numbers are in brackets [ ].*

a. [2] . . . most of <u>whose</u> mothers _____

b. [3] <u>It</u>'s a subtle but pervasive message_____

c. [3] To others, <u>the tradition</u> has long since shed that stigma . . .

_____

d. [4] She's conducted studies on <u>the subject</u> with her husband . . .

_____

e. [4] . . . <u>that</u>'s fine with them . . . _____

f. [6] Hillary Rodham Clinton went up against <u>those</u> attitudes in

Arkansas. _____

g. [8] . . . ways to create <u>that</u> bond. _____

h. [8] They said <u>their</u> software wouldn't take it. _____

i. [10] . . . even though <u>they</u> said they would do <u>it</u> for a woman.

_____

j. [11] . . . took his wife's name for <u>the same reason</u>.

_____

k. [14] . . . will have to figure <u>that one</u> out on their own.

_____

Reflect on Reading

In exercise 4 you looked for words that pronouns and demonstrative adjectives **refer** to. Many words refer to other words in a reading. For example:

They saw a sign on the highway. It said New York was 60 miles away.

In the second sentence, "it" refers to a word in the previous sentence. Is "it" the highway or the sign? You understand that "it" refers to the sign. Understanding **reference** is an important reading skill. Here are common reference words:

he, she, it, they	The car won't start. **It**'s stopped in the middle of the road.
	The Culbertsons couldn't be here tonight. **They** had another party to go to.
this, that, these, those	I stayed at a new hotel on the beach. **That** was the best part of my trip.
	The large boxes need to be opened. **Those** are the new computers.
one, another, the other, the first, the last, the former, the latter	There were two letters in the box. **The first/One** was from her parents. **The other** was an invitation to a party.
	We can deal with the problem in different ways. One way is to talk directly to Hanif. **Another** is to talk to Hanif's manager.
	Sonia tried two dating services, one she found on the Internet and one in the phone book. **The former** was awful, but she liked **the latter.**

5. *Find additional words from "Breaking with Tradition" that . . .*

describe a person's background	*religious,*
categorize groups of people	*couples,*
are related to types of attitudes	*sexist,*
are related to reporting research	*conducted studies,*
have meanings similar to these words	**a.** [1] something of no importance ___*a non-issue*___ **b.** [3,8] something that comes down to you from your family _____ **c.** [4] accepting of _____ **d.** [4] the standard of proper behavior _____ **e.** [7] to work very hard and long in order to get something _____ **f.** [8] things that are problems because they are difficult to work out _____ **g.** [10] the act of treating people differently and unfairly _____

6. *Discuss the following questions with a classmate.*

a. If a married woman changes her last name to her husband's, does she lose her identity? Is she more committed to her marriage than a woman who doesn't change her name?

b. Do nontraditional systems of naming cause confusion in society? Do they disrupt family life?

Quickwriting: Names

Quickwriting is a way to develop your ideas about a topic. Begin by writing your thoughts as quickly as you can. Don't worry about details like spelling, grammar, or punctuation. What is your opinion about whether women keep their own last names from birth when they get married? In your notebook, write for five to ten minutes about this topic.

Vocabulary Log

What words or phrases would you like to remember from this chapter? Write five to ten items in your notebook. Examples are on page 12.

Chapter 3

In Name Only

What things should parents consider when naming a child? In this chapter you will read about naming customs and write a description of your name.

Starting Point

Questions about Names

Naming a child is an important decision. How did your parents decide on your name?

Interview a classmate with these questions about his or her name.

1. Why were you given the name you have?
2. Does your name have a meaning?
3. How many names does a person in your culture have?
4. Do you have a nickname or an affectionate name among your family members or close friends?
5. Do you like your name? Would you like a different name? If so, what?

Reading 1

Naming Customs

There are interesting ways to name children in different countries of the world.

1. *Read the following selection.*

Naming Customs

[1] Cultures and families have different naming customs. An appropriate name can secure a child's future. In some Asian countries, parents go to a name fortune-teller or to a Buddhist priest to get a name that will bring good luck to a child. The number of strokes to write a child's name in Chinese, for example, will make a difference in that child's success in the future. In some places it is considered bad luck to give a girl a very strong name. People think this will bring her unhappiness in life and that girls should have names that are soft, cute, and beautiful. For example, in Japan, girls' names often end in *-ko*

(Akiko, Hiroko), which means "child." Chinese girls are often given names that mean "jade," "snow," or "flower." In the same way, boys should have names that are strong and suggest success and wealth. In Chinese, boys are given names like "brilliant" or "upright." It would not be good to give a boy a weak or feminine name.

[2]   Names can also indicate family genealogy or heritage. For example, in Korea, first names have two parts. The first part of a boy's first name usually follows a strict genealogy used for many generations. All the boys in one generation of a family, the brothers and male cousins, will have the same first part to their name. Similarly, in some Arabic-speaking countries, boys are given the first name of their paternal grandfather. In European countries, families may repeat the same names for several generations. In Iceland, a girl's last name translates as "daughter of . . ." and a boy's translates as "son of . . ."

[3]   Finally, some people name their children after famous people, for example, George Washington Carver. Others choose names of religious figures from the Bible. Names such as Joseph, Matthew, David, Ruth, Mary, and Sarah are biblical names. In this way, names may indicate the values of the family.

[4]   How much freedom do parents actually have to name their children? Customs are not the only things that restrict the naming of children. Some governments intervene to protect children from the names their parents want to give them. In Argentina, for example, names must be approved by the government. Parents cannot give their children strange or ridiculous names. Any foreign names must be Hispanicized. One couple wanted to call their child Kennedy but lost their case in court. In Germany, the government has the power to stop parents from giving their children strange names. Recent attempts to call children Bierstuebl ("Little Beer Hall") and Gott ("God") have not been accepted. One family fought to call their son Sascha, but the government insisted he have a middle name that showed that he was a boy. This is also an issue in Japan, where the government feels children should not be given names that other children will make fun of. One family fought unsuccessfully to name their child Akuma, which means "devil." Is naming exclusively a parental right? Should the government intervene? Whatever the government and parents decide, children have to live with their decisions!

ANSWER KEY

2. *Find other expressions in the selected paragraphs that have the same meaning as the expressions.*

Paragraph 1

a. bring good luck in life   *secure a child's future*

_____

b. bring bad luck   _____

Paragraph 4

c. stop parents from giving names _____

d. accepted   _____

e. fought unsuccessfully   _____

When you read, you use many different strategies to figure out vocabulary. You may try to guess from other information in the reading (the context). You may use your knowledge of related words, affixes, and word roots, or you may use your own knowledge of the subject. All of these strategies are part of the skill of **analyzing vocabulary** (see page 25).

3. **Analyze the vocabulary** in the reading. Try to guess what the word means. What strategy helped you to make this guess? Write your guess and the strategy in the chart.

ANSWER KEY

Word	Possible Meaning	Strategy (Context, Related Word, Word Root/Affix, Own Knowledge)
a. appropriate	good	context and own knowledge
b. secure	help make good	related word
c. strokes		
d. upright		
e. feminine		
f. strict		
g. genealogy		
h. paternal		
i. indicate		
j. Hispanicized		
k. parental		
l. intervene		

4. Which paragraph in the reading discusses the following naming customs?

ANSWER KEY

_____ showing family values

_____ hoping for good luck in life

_____ indicating genealogy

5. *Look at these sentences and decide which naming custom is being followed.* **Apply information** *from "Naming Customs."*

a. Both my grandfathers were named Joseph, my mother is Josephine, and my father and my brother are Robert Joseph, so I named my son Joseph.

_____

b. My first name is Hong Kab. My brother is called Hong Ki and my cousin is Hong Woon.

_____

c. They named their daughter Maria Jesus.

_____

d. My grandfather gave me my name because of my birth date. In the Thai zodiac, my name should have certain consonants and vowels in order to give me good luck.

_____

e. My grandfather's name was Farah Ali, my father's is Mustapha Farah, and my name is Farah Mustapha.

_____

f. Her name is Gudrunsdottir and her brother is Gudrunsson.

_____

g. My father gave me the names of two famous generals of North and South Korea because he hoped our countries would re-unite someday.

_____

h. When I was nine years old, my father went to a fortune-teller who changed my name because he felt it was not a lucky name for me.

_____

i. My grandfather named me for a famous banker because he hoped I would be a successful businessman.

_____

6. *Discuss these questions with a classmate:*

   a. Were you named according to one of the customs described in "Naming Customs"?

   b. Does your culture or family have any traditions for naming children? For example, when are children given names? Who gives the name? Is there a naming ceremony?

Reflect on Reading

If you understand what you read, you should be able to use the information in different situations. This is called **applying information.** You did this in exercise 5. This skill involves critical thinking—analyzing information or situations. In which of these situations would you need to apply information from your reading? Discuss with a classmate.

Reading the newspaper   Reading the directions to   Reading a recipe

---

Reading 2

Can dreams inspire names? This student essay tells how one woman got her name.

1. *Skim* *this selection to get the main idea of each paragraph. Then write the paragraph numbers in the blank beside the correct main idea.*

_____ Her feelings about her name in a different culture

_____ Meaning and reason for first name

_____ Her feelings about her name

_____ Common last names in her country

Too Beautiful to Love

ANSWER KEY

READING TIP

To get the main idea when you skim, read the first sentence of each paragraph. This sentence is often the main idea.

Too Beautiful to Love

[1]   My name is Mi-Ran Park. You can get an idea of my nationality from my last name. Park is one of the most common family names in Korea. Actually, more than 50 percent of the people have one of these three famous family names: Kim, Lee, and Park. According to a Korean legend, this is because we are descended from one original family 5,000 years ago.

[2]   From a very old tradition, almost every Korean name is written with Chinese letters. In Chinese, *Mi* means "beautiful" and *Ran* means "orchid." Therefore, my first name means a beautiful, fragrant flower. I was named by my mother from a dream she had when she was expecting me. In that dream, she bought three beautiful flowers and now she has three beautiful daughters. This is not a coincidence. My grandmother-in-law had a dream of four moons in the sky and then she had four daughters.

[3]   Some people feel that a flower name is not good even though flowers are beautiful. This is because a flower always needs a great deal of care or it will die. In fact, there is no flower that needs more care than an orchid. This is one reason that I dislike my name. I don't want to be a fragile, beautiful flower in a greenhouse, a flower that must be taken care of. I want to be a strong, independent woman.

Fortunately, I have another name, which is stronger and more energetic. My family calls me SuengWoon, which means "rising." I usually prefer to be called by this name rather than by Mi-Ran.

[4] Now that I'm in the United States, I am happy with the name Mi-Ran because I have never heard anyone say it incorrectly. Sometimes I even feel my name is more lovely when it is spoken in English than in Korean. I like that accent. At this time in my life, I thank my mother for having had an international sense when she gave me my name!

2. *Read the selection again to find* **specific information.** *For each item here, circle the number of the correct answer.*

ANSWER KEY

   a. Which of the following is NOT true?
     1. Mi-Ran was named by her grandmother.
     2. Mi-Ran was named for a flower in a dream.
     3. Mi-Ran's name means "beautiful orchid."
     4. Mi-Ran's mother got the idea for her name from a dream.

   b. Not everyone feels a flower name is a good name because
     1. women are fragile.
     2. it suggests strength.
     3. women are strong.
     4. it suggests weakness.

   c. Mi-Ran prefers the name her family calls her because
     1. it suggests strength and energy.
     2. it means "rising."
     3. she doesn't like the name Mi-Ran.
     4. it suggests beauty.

   d. According to Mi-Ran, Americans
     1. have trouble pronouncing her name.
     2. pronounce her name in a way she likes.
     3. have an international sense.
     4. are good at foreign names.

Targeting

Collocations for Describing Names

1. *Collocations are words that commonly go together. Study these collocations related to naming customs.*

Collocations	Examples
think of [a reason/name/occasion] **for** [someone or something]	We haven't **thought of** a name **for** the baby yet. I can't **think of** a reason **for** naming him that.
decide on [something]	Parents usually **decide on** their children's names themselves.
call/name [someone] [something]	They **named** their son Michael Jordan because they admired the basketball player so much. They always **call** me Meme at home.
give [someone] a name	My grandfather **gave** me my name.
name [someone] **after/for** [someone] [something]	I was **named after** my father's sister. Daisy was **named for** a flower.
change [something] **from** [one thing] **to** [something else]	As soon as she left home, she **changed** her name **from** Susie **to** Sarah.
use a nickname	Our teachers never **use** our nicknames.
go by [a different name]	I sometimes **go by** my maiden name. Other times I use my husband's name.
call [someone] **by** [a name]	We **call** her **by** her first name, but her family **calls** her **by** her middle name.

2. *Complete these collocations using the expressions in the chart on page 30. You may use the same word more than once.*

ANSWER KEY

I was _named after_ my mother because my parents couldn't
   (a)

_____ a better name for me. They were still arguing
       (b)

about what to _____ me on the way to the hospital.
                    (c)

My brother's name is Andrew, but almost everyone

_____ him Drew. My parents are the only ones who
       (d)

never _____ his nickname.
          (e)

My mother hated the name her parents _____
                                            (f)

her. When she was 18, she _____ her name
                               (g)

_____ Petunia _____ Patricia. She rarely

went _____ Petunia anyway. Most people
         (h)

_____ her Patty.
      (i)

3. *Rewrite these sentences using information about your name.*

a. My name means "stay beautiful, my daughter."

My name means _"Great and Tall Farmer," but the deeper_

meaning is "A Person of High Position."

b. My name comes from an old legend.

My name comes from _____ .

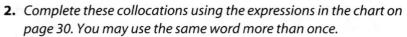

c. In my culture, people have a two-part first name and no middle name.

In my culture, people have _____ .

d. I like my name because it is unique. I have never met anyone else with this name.

I like my name because _____ .

OR

I don't like my name because _____ .

e. My mother named me after her two sisters.

_____ named me after

_____ .

f. I was named by a Buddhist priest.

I was named by _____ .

g. When I was young, I didn't like my name.

When I was young, _____ .

h. My name is very hard to pronounce in English.

My name _____ to pronounce in English.

i. My name is Abdulrahman, but my friends and family call me Abdul.

My name is _____ , but/and my friends

and family call me _____ .

It's usually a good idea to collect some ideas before you write. This practice can help organize your thoughts and keep you focused as you write.

Fill in this chart with details about your name.

Meaning of your name	
Naming customs in your family or culture	
Feelings about your name at different times in your life	
Experiences with your name at different times in your life	
Nicknames or names you would rather be called	

Your writing will be stronger and more interesting if you **provide support** for your ideas. You can use a variety of supporting techniques in your writing.

1. *Study the following common kinds of support.*

Kinds of Support	Examples
1. Stories, examples, specific details	When my mother and father learned that they were going to be parents of a boy, they went to a nice restaurant to celebrate and think about a good boy's name. They wanted a name that had meaning to both of their families and one that sounded good with my last name. They agreed to call me Robert because that name had been used in my mother's family for several generations. For a middle name, they chose my paternal grandfather's name, Nejat. They liked the meaning of the name: "all-knowing" and "freedom." It was also a way to honor my grandfather.
2. Facts, statistics, information from an authority	I like my family name, Li, but it is so common that I have met many people with the same last name. In fact, it is the most common last name in the world! In China, 87 million people have Li as a family name. Many people outside of China share the name Li, too.
3. Reasons, causes, and effects	Before the 1920s, people didn't have family names in Turkey. When the Ottoman Empire collapsed and Ataturk came to power, each family had to choose a last name. Because people always referred affectionately to my great-grandfather as "blue eyes," he chose that as our family name.

2. *Read each example. On the line, write the number of the kind of support from the chart in exercise 1. Some examples may use more than one kind of support.*

_____ **a.** When my parents named me, they considered several things. First, my last name is a common name in my hometown. If they gave me a common first name, I would share my name with many others, so they were careful about choosing a less common first name. Next, they considered the letters in my name because the correct number of strokes would give me good luck. Finally, they thought about the balance between my first and last name. Their names were simple to write, so they gave me complicated letters in my first name to go with my easy last name.

_____ **b.** My name is Abdulrahman. *Rahman* is one of the names of God and *Abdul* means "adore." Together they make a beautiful name, "to adore God."

_____ **c.** I have always had two names, an Indonesian one and a Chinese one. This is not unusual in Indonesia. But after I was nine years old, my father changed my names because a fortune-teller said that my names were not good for me. This fortune-teller gave me a new Indonesian and a new Chinese name. They had some meaning, but I quickly forgot them because I didn't like my new names. They sounded very strange to my ears. My family and neighbors continued to call me by my nickname, San, because they, too, could not change their habits. Someday, I will officially change to my old Chinese name, which I always liked.

_____ **d.** It is a custom in my country for the paternal grandfather to name babies, but this was not the case when I was born. Because I was the third of three daughters, my paternal grandfather was so unhappy that he did not go to the hospital to see me, and he refused to name me. Instead, my maternal grandfather gave me my name and for that reason, I loved him greatly and disliked my father's father. When my favorite grandfather died, I was still a child. I was depressed for a year and hardly spoke to anyone. I couldn't explain why. No one seemed to understand how important it was that he had loved me enough to give me a name.

_____ **e.** In the United States, most people give their children a first and a middle name. Names are usually chosen because of the sound or to remember someone in the family.

3. *Go back to your chart in Preparing to Write 1 on page 33. In the margin, write some notes about kinds of support you could add to these ideas about your name.*

Writing a Description of Your Name

Write a description of your name. Use expressions from Targeting: Collocations for Describing Names on page 30 and your notes from the Preparing to Write exercises to help you.

> **WRITING TIP**
>
> Give lots of details so that the reader will understand your description.

Editing and Rewriting

Editing for Verb Tense Errors

Always reread your writing to check for correct use of verb tenses. Look for time clues that show the need for the past or future tense.

1. *Study the rules on page 37.*

Rules	Examples
Use the present tense for habits, facts, and general truths.	She **likes** her name because it is very feminine. My friends **call** me Tiger because I am very strong.
Be careful with subject-verb agreement in the present tense. Check for singular subjects. Don't forget to add the final -s to the verb that follows a third person singular subject.	Everyone calls me Bea instead of Beatrice. Confusion about names causes a lot of problems.
Use the simple past tense for facts and events that happened in the past.	My father **named** me after his father. When I was young, I **didn't like** my name, but now I do.
Use the present perfect for facts and events that happened in the past, are continuing now, or may happen again.	I **have** always **loved** my name. My paternal grandfather **has named** all of his grandchildren.
Use the simple future (**will** + verb) or (**be going to** + verb) to talk about events in the future.	I **am going to change** my last name when I get married. I love my name. I **will** never **change** it.

For information about irregular past tense verbs and changing the tenses of verbs, see Reference, page 243.

2. *Correct the verb tense errors in the following sentences. Not all sentences have mistakes.*

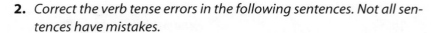

  a. My grandfather named me for a rich man who ~~is~~ famous dur-
      ing my grandfather's time.

  b. At home, my family always calls me Petie, and I like that nick-
      name.

  c. When I was in elementary school, my teachers call me by my
      last name.

  d. All my life I always love my name.

  e. I recently change my name because I got married.

  f. I want a name that expressed my personality better.

  g. When I was born, my father give me a Chinese name, but I like
      my Indonesian name better.

  h. After I was nine years old, my father change my Indonesian
      name.

  i. I didn't like my new name. It sounds very strange to me.

  j. Maybe in the future I change my name.

3. *Correct the underlined verb tense and subject-verb agreement errors in the following paragraph.*

Last year South Korea's highest court <u>strike</u> down a 689-year-

                                                             (a)

old law that <u>prevent</u> people with the same surname from marry-

                   (b)

ing one another. The court <u>rule</u> that it <u>will be</u> unconstitutional

                                      (c)   (d)

and outdated.

The recent decision <u>affect</u> an estimated 60,000 couples who

                                          (e)

<u>lived</u> together but whose clan names <u>keep</u> them from marrying,

 (f)   (g)

even though there <u>has been</u> no evidence of blood ties.
(h)

The law <u>is written</u> in 1308, when inbreeding <u>is</u> a concern
(i) (j)

because people <u>live</u> in isolated villages for generations.
(k)

Editing Checklist

Check the Content

1. *Exchange your description with a classmate. After you read your classmate's description, answer this question:*

   ❑ Are there enough details?

Check the Details

2. *Read your own description again. If necessary, revise your description. Add or change details. Then continue checking your description. Use these questions:*

   ❑ Is the present tense used for habits, facts, or general truths? Check for subject-verb agreement.
   ❑ Is the simple past used for facts and events that happened in the past?
   ❑ Is the present perfect used for facts or events that happened in the past but are related to now?
   ❑ Is the future used for events that will happen in the future?

3. *Revise your writing.*

Vocabulary Log

What words or phrases would you like to remember from this chapter? Write five to ten items in your notebook. Examples are on page 12.

Grammar and Punctuation Review

Look over your writing for this chapter. What changes did you need to make in grammar and punctuation? Write them in your notebook. Review them before the next writing assignment.

Class Activity   Name Booklet

1 Read your classmates' papers about their names.

2 Mark the part of each paper that you like the best. The passage can be about the meaning of the name, how the person got the name, or any other detail.

3 When you get your paper back, decide which part you want to put in the class booklet. You don't have to choose one that your classmates marked.

4 Put all of the passages into one class booklet in any format the class chooses. You might want to add some art that shows how students write their names in their languages or that illustrates the meaning of some names.

2 Food for Thought

You often make choices about food and follow certain rules about eating without giving them a second thought. What do these choices say about you? How are your snacking customs and table manners different from others around the world? What kinds of restaurants do you like?

These are some of the activities you will do in this unit:

- **Read about food cravings**
- **Read about favorite "munchies" around the world**
- **Create a chart listing typical snacks**
- **Read about mealtime customs in different countries**
- **Write a guide to mealtime customs**
- **Read about restaurants**
- **Write a restaurant review**

Chapter 4

Cravings

Do you ever have a *craving* for a certain kind of food? Most people do. Are cravings different depending on your mood? Do cravings differ for men and women? Read on to find out!

Starting Point

What Do You Crave?

A craving is an intense desire for something. People often experience cravings for certain kinds of food.

Discuss these questions with a partner or a small group:

1. Many people in the United States snack (eat between meals). Do you?

2. What snack food would be most difficult for you to live without?

Comfort Food Cravings

According to this selection, cravings are caused by more than just hunger!

1. *Read the following selection. Find out what various kinds of cravings say about you. Some of the words in the first paragraph are **slang,** or playful words often used for humor.*

Comfort Food Cravings

[1]   Do you crave crunchies when you get the munchies? Cheer yourself up with chocolate? Chill out with ice cream? A recent survey of Americans' eating habits shows that people snack for the sake of their spirits as well as for their stomachs.

[2]   Why do you choose the foods you do? The answer involves a lot more than appetite. "For us humans, eating is never a 'purely biological' activity," observes Sidney Mintz, author of *Tasting Food, Tasting Freedom.*

> **READING TIP**
>
> Don't worry about words that are unfamiliar to you. Just keep reading for the general meaning.

[3] Foods from "the four basic snack food groups"—bready, crunchy, creamy, and chewy—fill different sensory and emotional needs, according to Julie Kembel, author of *Winning the Weight and Wellness Game*.

[4] Crunch is the secret to chips' soaring popularity, points out Kembel. "We tend to store tension in our jaws, so when we eat something crunchy, we tense and relax our jaws, relieving some of that ache." Chewy foods with carbohydrates, like bagels or licorice, help you slow down and unwind. Bready foods, like puddings, pasta, and porridge, create a feeling of fullness that makes you feel more secure. Finally, creamy foods—luscious objects of sensory delight—are "our way of . . . indulging ourselves," adds Kembel.

[5] When you're feeling down or distressed, you probably yearn for more than a mouthful of something nutritious or delicious. However, there's a definite gender difference in choosing comfort foods. Nearly half of the women surveyed (49 percent) prefer chocolate, while ice cream soothes the souls and stomachs of about four in 10 men (43 percent). From a nutritional standpoint, these foods have a lot in common. "Chocolate and ice cream are similar in fat and sugar composition and in biological effects," notes Debra Waterhouse, author of *Why Women Need Chocolate*. "Both release brain chemicals—serotonin and endorphins—that make us feel better."

(ANSWER KEY)

2. *Find a word or phrase in the reading that means . . .*

Paragraph 1
a. feelings of hunger (*slang*)   _____

b. make yourself feel happier   _____

c. make yourself more relaxed
(*slang*)   _____

d. eat a small meal in between
regular meals   _____

Paragraph 2
e. a feeling of hunger   _____

Paragraph 3
f. related to the senses of touch,
taste, and feel   _____

Paragraph 4

g. increasing quickly   _____

h. strain   _____

i. delicious   _____

j. allowing a special pleasure   _____

Paragraph 5

k. depressed   _____

l. have a strong desire for   _____

m. healthy to eat   _____

n. male or female   _____

o. calms   _____

p. point of view   _____

q. brain chemicals   _____

3. *Complete the statements about "Comfort Food Cravings." Circle the number of the best answer. The answers may not be directly stated in the reading. You may have to **infer** the meaning.*

    (ANSWER KEY)

a. Someone who is hungry for something crunchy is

probably _____ .

    1. tense   **2.** relaxed   **3.** self-indulgent

b. If you have had a busy day and need to calm down, you may

find _____ food satisfying.

    1. crunchy   **2.** chewy   **3.** bready

c. Ice cream and chocolate comfort people because of _____ .

    1. gender differences   **2.** chemical reactions   **3.** nutrition

d. If you told the experts quoted in this story that you had a

craving, they would probably say, _____ .

    1. "Why are you hungry? Didn't you have lunch?"

    2. "I wonder why you feel this craving right now."

    3. "Chocolate always makes everyone feel better."

    e. A man who is feeling unhappy may crave _____ .
        1. ice cream   **2.** chocolate   **3.** bready foods

    f. This article is true for _____ .
        1. people all over the world
        2. people in North America
        3. people in the United States

    g. A craving for food is _____ need.
        1. an emotional
        2. a biological
        3. both an emotional and a biological

4. *How about you? Do you ever have cravings for these kinds of foods? Write an example and circle* **yes** *or* **no.**

		Yes	No
Crunchy foods?	Example: _____	Yes	No
Bready foods?	Example: _____	Yes	No
Creamy foods?	Example: _____	Yes	No
Chewy foods?	Example: _____	Yes	No

Reading 2

The Food Pyramid

How healthy is the diet of the U.S. population? According to the government, people will get adequate nutrition if they follow official food recommendations.

1. *Read the following selection.*

The Food Pyramid

[1] With more fresh food available year-round, one might think that everyone's diet would improve. However, this is clearly not the case as more and more people eat food that is far from fresh and far from

healthy. According to Grolier's online edition of the *Academic American Encyclopedia*, in the United States, about 40% of the calories that people consume come from fat and about 20% come from sugar. Fat and sugar crowd out other, more nutritious foods. This can lead to deficiencies in iron, calcium, complex carbohydrates, and fibers—which in turn can cause a number of health problems.

[2]   For many years the United States Department of Agriculture (USDA) issued dietary guidelines based on four basic food groups: meat and meat substitutes, fruits and vegetables, milk and dairy products, and grains, including bread and cereals. The USDA declared that a balanced diet would include at least one food from each group in each meal every day. However, in 1980 the government began to recommend that people eat a greater variety of foods daily, including these categories: fruits; vegetables; whole and enriched grain products; dairy products; meats, poultry, fish, eggs; and dried peas and beans. This variety of foods is necessary to prevent a deficiency or an excess of any one nutrient.

[3]   In 1992 the government changed the daily diet recommendations from four equal food groups, represented in a square, to five food groups represented in a pyramid. Foods at the top of the pyramid—fats, oils, and sweets—should be eaten only sparingly. People need protein in moderate amounts in their diets, so the upper middle section of the pyramid contains two groups of food that supply protein: milk, yogurt, and cheese; and meat, poultry, fish, dried beans, eggs, and nuts. Nutritionists recommend that people eat two to three servings of these foods a day. Most Americans need to eat more fruits and vegetables, represented in the two lower middle sections of the pyramid. People should eat three to five servings of vegetables and two to four servings of fruit. The base of the pyramid consists of grains, the food group that should be eaten the most (six to eleven servings a day), including bread, cereals, rice, and pasta. When people follow the recommendations in the food pyramid, they will eat a wide variety of food items that will provide them with the right proportion of nutrients.

2. ***Taking notes in diagram form*** *can help you understand a reading. It is also a useful way to take notes for courses because diagrams are easy to refer to later. Complete the charts with information from the reading.*

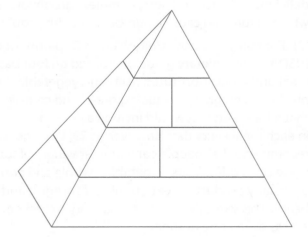

3. ***Apply information*** *from the reading. Compare your typical diet with the recommendations in the food pyramid. How is it similar or different?*

_____

_____

4. *Read each pair of sentences. Which sentence in each pair is specific? Which is general? Write **S** or **G** on the blank lines.*

a. _____ Many people eat food that is far from fresh and far from healthy.

_____ About 40% of the calories that people consume come from fat and about 20% come from sugar.

b. _____ People should eat three to five servings of vegetables and two to four servings of fruit.

_____ People need to eat more fruits and vegetables, represented in the two lower middle sections of the pyramid.

READING TIP

The main idea of a paragraph or reading is usually the most general idea. Specific details support the main idea. When you look for the main idea, decide which ideas are specific and which are more general.

c. _____ In 1980 the government began to recommend that people eat a greater variety of foods daily, including these categories: fruits; vegetables; whole and enriched grain products; dairy products; meats, poultry, fish, eggs; and dried peas and beans.

_____ This variety of foods is necessary to prevent a deficiency or an excess of any one nutrient.

d. _____ In 1992 the government changed the daily diet recommendations from four equal food groups, represented in a square, to five food groups, represented in a pyramid.

_____ Foods at the top of the pyramid—fats, oils, and sweets—should be eaten only sparingly.

5. *If you know common endings for different* **word forms,** *you can improve your reading. Find words in "The Food Pyramid" to complete this chart.*

Verb	Noun	Adjective
improve	*improvement*	*improved*
	health	
		deficient
diet		
govern		
		recommended
	variety	various
	day	
		nutritious

Reading 3

World's TV Watchers Favor Assorted Munchies

READING TIP

Definitions are often set off from the rest of the sentence by parentheses or commas. Occasionally they are explained in the sentence that follows the word.

For many people, watching sports on TV is an occasion for a snack. This selection reports on favorite TV snacks for people around the world.

1. *Read the following selection. When you see unfamiliar words, look for a definition in the reading before you look in a dictionary.*

World's TV Watchers Favor Assorted Munchies

[1] When an important sports event takes place, millions of people all over the world gather in front of their TVs to watch it. Some watch the event by themselves; others invite friends over to make it a social occasion. A lot of these people take their eyes off the TV only to reach out for a snack. What is the favorite food for TV watchers?

[2] In Canada, people eat plenty of chips and salsa, but in Ottawa they eat something called a beaver tail. Maple syrup covers fried dough in the shape of a beaver tail. In Calgary, people might entertain their TV guests with some steaks, washed down with a strong local beer called a Big Rock Magpie. Middle-class French Canadians in Quebec sometimes like to prepare a batch of *poutine*, a combination of French fries, brown gravy, and curd cheese. Upper-class people from Quebec eat it, too, but they don't admit it.

[3] What Mexicans eat in front of the TV depends on what they're watching. When they watch soccer on TV, it's usually at a neighborhood cantina, where they drink beer, rum, tequila, or a mix of brandy and cola. Once everyone is starving, waiters bring in food from the kitchen—free! The first course is often *carnitas* (fried pork cutlets) and *chicharrón* (fried pork skin). The main fare is usually *pozole*, a pork broth with a floating hunk of corn on the cob, or *menudo*, a stew of cow stomach and chile, often fiery hot.

[4] When something special happens on TV, Russians celebrate with vast quantities of icy vodka. There is a class system, of course. Poor people drink $2 bottles with names like "Russian Vodka" that can be bought on any street corner. People who have a little money drink the best Russian brands—Smirnov, Moskovskoye, or Stolichnaya. Rich people drink Absolut or American Smirnoff—anything foreign.

[5] Sitting in front of the TV to watch the triumphs of German tennis players or soccer teams, Germans seem to favor snacks like salted,

slender pretzel sticks or *Erdnussflips*. These are small, light brown, peanut-flavored corn snacks.

[6] "Oh, it's beer, lots of beer," says Wandie Ndala, naming the refreshment of choice for South African TV watchers. Hungry township sports fans might order pap and mutton (pap is the country's staple corn mash) or even pap and *amathumbu* (cow stomach) during a soccer match. While drinking preferences appear to be the same for sports lovers across race and class lines in South Africa, snacking preferences are not. "The beer is the same, but the food is predominantly bar-type munchies—chips and snacks," says Darren Heath. Heath manages a pub in a wealthy, white suburb in Johannesburg that offers big-screen TV for soccer, rugby, and cricket matches.

[7] British television snackers prefer tea with chocolates or chocolate biscuits (cookies), beer or wine with potato chips or nuts, and occasionally cheese and crackers. Some people like their nibbles with dips, while the health-conscious can opt for one of the many low-fat crisps (chips).

[8] The French rarely snack. Even the word for snack—*grignoter* —is a negative word. "The vagabond eater is still frowned upon," notes Claude Fischler, an expert on food at the National Center for Scientific Research. Although the French seldom bring snacks to the TV, they increasingly bring the TV to the table. A survey by the dairy industry showed that 62 percent of meals are eaten with the TV on. A major sporting event is needed to shift the focus of eating from the table to the television couch. Once there, spectators eat baguettes (French bread) with Camembert, pate, cold pork sausages, and roast chicken—all accompanied by free-flowing red wine.

2. *Answer these questions about the reading:*

   a. In paragraph 1, find a word or phrase that means . . .

      1. happens   _____

      2. get together _____

   b. In paragraph 2, underline the definitions of beaver tail and *poutine*. Do upper-class people in Quebec eat *poutine*?

      _____

   c. Find the word "cantina" in paragraph 3. What do you think it means?

      _____

d. In paragraph 3, find four typical snacks served in Mexico. Underline their definitions.

e. How many classes of people does the author talk about in Russia in paragraph 4? _____

f. Underline the definition of an *Erdnussflip* in paragraph 5.

g. Do all people in South Africa share a preference for beer? How about a preference for snacks? Check paragraph 6.

_____

h. From the reading, what can you **infer** about the author's attitude toward alcohol? Which one of these two statements does the author seem to believe?

1. Drinking alcohol is not acceptable even though it is common.

2. Drinking quite a bit of alcohol is acceptable and common.

Reflect on Reading	In "World's TV Watchers Favor Assorted Munchies," the writer gives a lot of definitions. Look back at the reading. How can you recognize a definition? Discuss your answer with a classmate.

Writing

Preparing to Write: Designing a Chart

Sometimes a **chart** is the clearest way to present information. As students and in your work life, you will probably need to present information in chart form. This section provides practice in creating a chart and writing a paragraph of introduction for it.

1. *Put information about snacking habits into a chart. Follow these steps:*

a. Reread "Comfort Food Cravings" and "World's TV Watchers Favor Assorted Munchies." What information would be easy to show in a chart? What would be a good title for this chart?

_____

b. Decide what the columns and rows will be in your chart. Write some categories here.

c. Find out information about snacks in two or three other countries to include in your chart.

d. Charts rarely stand alone. They need an introduction to give readers background information and interest them in the topic. What information does a reader need to know about your chart? Is there a "catchy" way to interest the reader in this topic? Write a short introduction to the chart (one or two sentences).

_____

_____

Writing a Chart

WRITING TIP

If you use any symbols, abbreviations, or colors in your chart, consider using a legend or key to explain them.

Now put together all your information from Preparing to Write in a chart with an introduction and title. Write your chart information in a consistent form. Remember that too much detail can make your chart difficult to read.

Editing and Rewriting

Editing for Consistency in Charts and Lists

One of the biggest problems with charts and lists is presenting the information in a consistent form. Each element in the chart or list needs to have the same structure and format.

1. *Study this information about being consistent in charts.*

Consistency in . . .	*Examples*
Structure	They wanted to **eat, listen** to music, and **relax.** When you diet, focus on: • **eating** less • **changing** your attitude about food • **exercising** more
Format	Type of food

Meat	Vegetable	Fruit
• beef	• corn	• apple
• chicken	• squash	• pear
• pork	• broccoli	• peach

Punctuation and Capitalization	The menu lacks variety: Appetizers—few choices Entrées—too many cream sauces Desserts—limited to cake and ice cream

2. *Correct the problems with consistency in the following lists and charts.*

a. Do you have sensitive teeth, ~~suffering from~~ cold sores, or chapped lips? There is probably a simple remedy for your problems in your kitchen.

b. These simple remedies can help you
- look better
- improve your health
- relaxation

c. To get rid of a wart, tape a piece of raw eggplant on it, keep the eggplant on overnight, and repeating this every night.

d.

Problem	Home Remedy	*modern remedy*
warts	eggplant	chemical solution

e. To freshen your breath,
- some sorbet
- try some orange rind
- eat parsley

f.

Day 1	Day Two	Day 3
2200 calories	2000 calories	1800 calories

g. Instead of buying a facial mask, try using
- oatmeal and rosemary
- Cucumbers on Your Eyelids
- grapes and champagne

h. A treatment with mayonnaise may help dry hair. There are three steps to the process:
1. Spread a small amount of mayonnaise on your hair.
2. Wrap your head with plastic wrap for 30 minutes
3. Shampoo your hair.

3. *Make the problems in the first column consistent. Then fill in the remedies with your own ideas. Be careful about being consistent!*

Kitchen-Cupboard Remedies	
Problem	*Remedy*
Depression	*Eat two bananas every day.*
Have colds	_____
If you have bad breath	_____
INSECT BITES OR STINGS	_____
Wrinkles on Your Face	_____
Puffy Eyes	_____
(Your ideas)	_____

Editing Checklist

Check the Content

1. *Exchange your chart with a classmate. After you read your classmate's chart, answer these questions:*

   ❑ Do the title and introduction help you understand what the chart is about?
   ❑ Is the chart complete and easy to read?

Check the Details

2. *Now, reread your chart. If necessary, revise it. Add more explanation or reword some information. Then continue checking your writing. Use these questions:*

   ❑ Is all the information in the chart consistent—all nouns or all verbs, for example?
   ❑ Did you use consistent capitalization and punctuation?

3. *Revise your writing.*

Vocabulary Log

What words or phrases would you like to remember from this chapter? Write five to ten items in your notebook. Examples are on page 12.

Chapter 5

Mind Your Manners!

Different dining customs are fun to read and talk about. You will also have an opportunity to write about your dining customs in this chapter.

Starting Point

Mealtime Customs

Customs in restaurants and at the dinner table vary widely from country to country.

Discuss these questions with a partner or a small group:

1. Do you have guests to dinner very often? Is it more common for people to have friends come to dinner at home or to meet them in restaurants?

2. If you are invited to someone's house for dinner, do you take a gift? Do you send something before dinner? What is appropriate for a gift?

3. What time do you usually eat dinner?

4. Do people talk while eating or wait until they have finished eating to have a conversation?

5. Where would a special guest sit at the table? Facing the door? At the head of the table? On the right of the host? On the left? In the middle position at the side of the table?

6. At a restaurant, which of these methods would you use to get a server's attention? Put checks (✓) next to your choices.

   Snap your fingers. _____

   Curl your first finger and move it toward you. _____

   Motion with your palm down and your fingers curled toward you. _____

   Clap your hands. _____

   Make a kissing noise. _____

   Make a whistling or hissing noise. _____

   Raise your hand and call out. _____

   Raise your hand and make eye contact. _____

Raise your hand with your first finger raised. _____

Catch the waiter's eye and move your head backward quickly. _____

Catch the waiter's eye and move your head down toward the table. _____

....

The following selection presents various table manners and mealtime customs from around the world.

1. *Long readings sometimes need headings such as the following to help focus the reader. As you read this selection, **identify the topic** of each section. Write an appropriate heading on each blank line.*

Leaving Food or Not

Observing Carefully

Keeping Your Hands in the Right Place

Using a Toothpick

Eating Internationally

Serving Something to Drink

Using Tableware

Cleaning Hands

All Manner of Manners

[1]   The Parker Pen Company has been doing business internationally since 1902. In that time, the company has collected many reports about customs in different countries. In 1985, Parker Pen asked Roger Axtell, one of its international sales representatives, to collect these reports in a book about cultural differences. The result is a series of books called *Do's and Taboos Around the World*.

---

[2]   The books deal with all sorts of customs, but the information about eating gives an idea of the challenges an international traveler faces. Customs for dining with guests vary so much from one country to another that you could do something polite in one country that has a completely different meaning in another. Here is one classic example: a host in the United States offers a guest from Jordan more food at dinner. The guest refuses and the host does not offer again. The Jordanian may be shocked and hungry because in Jordan, it is polite for the host to offer the food several times while it is polite for guests to refuse, even if they want more. Then what happens when someone from Jordan travels to Zambia? There, according to Axtell, it is impolite for the host to offer food first. If you aren't aware of this custom, you may all be hungry!

---

[3]   In some countries, guests are expected to finish everything on their dinner plates. In other countries, such as Egypt, it is polite to leave something. In China, the host will continue to fill a guest's dish. It is polite to leave some food in the dish in order to show how generous the host was. At a formal dinner, the second-to-last course is sometimes plain boiled rice. You should refuse this to show that you are satisfied and full.

---

[4]   What about serving yourself more to drink? In many Asian countries, you can fill everyone else's glasses, but not your own. You will have to wait for someone else to offer you more to drink. However, if you are a woman in Italy, don't pour your neighbor a glass. Some people do not consider this appropriate behavior for a woman. If you do pour the wine, think twice about which hand you use. In Bolivia and Chile, most people consider it incorrect to pour the wine with

your left hand. When someone pours you something to drink, do you hold your glass up or leave it on the table? Customs for this are different in many countries.

––––––––––––––––––––

[5] In the United States, you are supposed to keep one hand in your lap while you're eating. It is considered impolite to put your elbows on the table. Diners usually hold a knife and fork only when they are cutting something, and then they put the knife down to change hands and eat with the fork in their right hand. If food is fairly soft, they use the side of the fork to cut it. However, in many countries, just the opposite is often true. People eat with their wrists resting on the edge of the table and continue to hold both the knife and the fork in their hands while they eat. In Brazil, it is considered rude to cut food with the side of a fork.

––––––––––––––––––––

[6] According to Axtell, if you want more food in Spain, you should put your knife and fork down on opposite sides of the plate. In Greece, to show that you are finished, cross your knife and fork on the plate with the fork facing up underneath. In Argentina, do the same thing, but put the fork face down. In other countries, you position your knife and fork close together on the side of the plate or diagonally when you are finished.

[7] Of course, in many countries people don't eat with knives and forks. They may eat with their hands, but in most countries only with the *right* hand. The left hand is considered unclean. If people use chopsticks, it is common to pick up the dish and hold it close to your mouth. But how close should you hold it? Customs vary from country to country!

––––––––––––––––––––

[8] In some countries, cleaning your hands is part of the mealtime experience. In Morocco, someone will bring a pitcher of water and a basin before you eat. You hold your hands over the basin and rinse your hands in the water that is poured from the pitcher. In Japan, you will get a warm, wet cloth to wipe your hands before you eat. In other countries, such as Italy, cleaning your hands *after* you eat is important. You may have a finger bowl beside your plate to rinse your fingers in.

[9] When you have finished eating, can you use a toothpick? In the United States, it is impolite to use a toothpick in public. In other countries, using a toothpick shows that the food was delicious. But be careful how you use the toothpick! In some countries, it is polite to hide the toothpick behind your hand.

[10] So what is a traveler to do? Axtell recommends that you watch others carefully to see what *they* do. He also says that conversations about customs are very interesting, so ask questions about ways to do things. He ends each of his books by talking about the universal action that can help a traveler in many situations—the smile.

2. ***Taking notes*** *as you read can help you remember information. Take notes from "All Manner of Manners" about table manners. Then fill in the chart.*

Country	Custom

Country	Custom

3. *Can you add any other customs that are not mentioned in "All Manner of Manners"?*

Country	Custom

Targeting

Ways to Give Advice   You can give advice in a variety of ways.

1. *Study these expressions that are often used to give advice.*

Expressions	Examples
You **should(n't)** [verb]	You **should** wait to ask for more food.
You **need to** [verb]	You **need to** wait before you begin eating.
Be careful (not) to [verb]	**Be careful not to** pour wine with the wrong hand.
Be careful about "had better." It is usually used when people in authority are giving advice to someone who has less power.	
It's [adjective] **to** [verb] or **[verb + ing]** is [adjective]	**It's** impolite **to** speak while you eat. . **Saying** thank you is important.
begin/start [verb + ing]	Don't **start** eating until your hostess picks up her fork.
wait/begin/start to [verb]	The best idea is to **wait to** see what other people are doing.

2. *Correct the errors in the following advice expressions.*

   a. In Jordan, if you want more food, you should to refuse the first time your host offers you more to eat. It is impolite ask for more yourself.

    b. In a formal dinner in China you ought to refusing the rice at the end of the meal.

    c. Be careful not use your left hand to serve someone in the Middle East.

    d. If you want more to eat in Spain, you should putting your knife and fork on opposite sides of the plate.

    e. Guests usually wait see what their host will order in a restaurant before they decide what to order themselves.

    f. If your hosts offer you more, it is difficult decide what to say.

    g. If you begin to filling your own glass, people may think that is rude.

3. *Complete these sentences with information about customs you know of that are related to table manners.*

    a. You shouldn't _____ .

    b. Be careful not to _____ .

    c. It's _____ to _____ .

    d. _____ is more polite than _____ .

    e. Don't start _____ .

    f. When you are _____ , wait _____ .

Writing

Preparing to Write: Clustering Ideas

Table manners differ from culture to culture, but they sometimes also differ from home to public places. What are the "rules" in your family or in your culture for polite behavior at the table in public places?

1. *Imagine that you have been asked to write a description of table manners that are considered polite or impolite in your country. This information will appear in a guide for people traveling in your country. First, write the place or situation on the top line of the chart in exercise 2 that follows.*

2. *Make notes in the following chart about the "Do's" and "Don't's" of table manners. Write as many things as possible on the topic. Work quickly and don't worry about exact words or complete sentences.*

(place or situation)

Do	*Don't*

3. *Read your notes in exercise 2 again. What ideas might be most interesting to write about? Circle these. Draw lines to connect any related ideas in the circles.*

4. *Take a few minutes to think about what you want to write. Will you write about a variety of table manners or just one? Write a sentence here to introduce your ideas.*

_____

_____

Writing about Customs

Use your ideas from Preparing to Write to write a guide about table manners. Provide lots of details. Use some paragraph headings to make your information easier to read.

WRITING TIP

In a travel guide, your writing should be impersonal. Avoid using *I, we, my,* and *our.* It's all right to use *you.*

Editing for Gerunds and Infinitives

It is sometimes confusing to know when to use gerunds and infinitives.

1. *Study the following information.*

Rules	Examples
A **gerund** is a verb form that ends in *-ing*.	**eating, pouring**
An **infinitive** is the base form of the verb following *to*.	**to eat, to pour**
Both gerunds and infinitives can be used as the subjects of sentences.	**Pointing** your knife at someone is rude. **To point** your knife at someone is rude.
It is more common to use a "false subject," **it,** with infinitives.	**It** is rude **to point** your knife at someone.
Infinitives may show purpose.	I wrote a thank-you note **to express** my thanks. **To show** her thanks, she sent them a present.
Gerunds may be used as nouns following prepositions.	Be careful **about refusing** something.
Gerunds and infinitives also follow verbs.	He enjoys **eating** French food. He likes **to eat** French food.

For more information about which verbs take gerunds or infinitives, see pages 240–242 in the Reference section.

2. *Underline all the gerunds and infinitives in the following sentences. Write a **G** above the gerunds and an **I** above the infinitives.*

      I

  a. <u>To show</u> thanks in China, people sometimes rap their fingers lightly on the table.

  b. People sometimes make a "fingertip kiss" to show appreciation for something.

  c. Eating with your mouth open is considered rude in most countries.

  d. Burping shows that you are pleasantly full.

  e. In some places, it is impolite to burp.

  f. If you aren't interested in eating more, leave some food on your plate to show that you don't need any more.

  g. Is it customary to change hands after you use a knife and fork to cut your food, or is it okay to keep the fork in your left hand while you eat?

  h. In the United States, it is polite to keep one hand in your lap when you eat. In France, having both hands visible is more polite. I remember hearing one time that the custom of keeping your hands visible to others at the table was related to safety in the old days. People felt better when they knew that someone wasn't holding a knife or gun under the table!

3. *Correct errors in the following paragraph. Some sentences may be correct.*

    (a) To teaching children to be polite when they eat is very important. **(b)** It is really boring for children to learning good manners. **(c)** I remember have pretend "tea parties" with my mother when I was young. **(d)** This was her way of show us how to behave at the table. **(e)** It was also fun learn in this way. **(f)** It is difficult for children to understanding the importance of good manners.

(g) However, when they are older, they will appreciate not having
to worry about manners at the table.

Editing Checklist

Check the Content

1. *Exchange your dining customs guide with a classmate. After you read your class-mate's information, answer these questions:*

   ❑ Is it clear to you what is polite and what is impolite?
   ❑ Is any information missing?

Check the Details

2. *Now, reread your dining customs guide. If necessary, revise your information. Add more details. Then continue checking your own writing. Use these questions:*

   ❑ Find any gerunds or infinitives. Did you use the right form?
   ❑ Check your verb forms for correct subject-verb agreement and tense.
   ❑ Are all the sentences complete?

3. *Revise your writing.*

Vocabulary Log

What words or phrases would you like to remember from this chapter? Write five to ten items in your notebook. Examples are on page 12.

Grammar and Punctuation Review

Look over your writing from this chapter. What changes did you need to make in grammar and punctuation? Write them in your notebook. Review them before the next writing assignment.

Chapter 6

Going Out to Eat

What kind of restaurants do you like to go to? In this chapter you will find out about an unusual kind of restaurant, read a review of a restaurant, and write your own restaurant review.

Starting Point

Choosing a Restaurant

People choose restaurants according to the kind of food they prefer, how much money they want to spend, and a lot of other reasons! What makes you decide to try a new restaurant?

Look at the photographs below. Which of the restaurants would you choose to eat in? Why?

A restaurant review gives information about a restaurant as well as the writer's opinion about it.

1. *From the title, "Bugs Part of the Cure," and the photograph, **predict** what kind of restaurant you think this selection discusses.*

_____

2. *Now think of what the selection may include. Make some **predictions** about its content.*

<u>kind of food</u>   _____   _____

_____   _____   _____

3. *Read the following selection. As you read, think about whether your predictions were correct.*

Bugs Part of the Cure

[1] The Imperial Herbal Restaurant in Singapore has attracted attention all over the world because of its unusual menu and approach to food.

[2] The restaurant has its own doctor, Li Lian Xing, a Chinese herbal physician. Dr. Li is also a pharmacist, and he is certified to prescribe food for health. When he's not working out recipes for the chef, Dr. Li offers diners free medical check-ups and sells herbal medicines.

[3] The menu lists the health benefits of each selection. For example, red plum drink "reduces the body's heat, dilates the blood vessels, reduces cholesterol, and helps digest meat," restaurant owner Wang-Lee Tee Eng told a writer from *Gourmet* magazine. Dr. Li held the writer's hand and prescribed chicken stir-fried with gingko nuts to lower his body temperature.

[4] Although this approach to dining may not sound like everyone's cup of tea, everything on the menu is delicious. The restaurant is so popular that it doesn't even have to advertise. Located in Singapore's central hotel district, the restaurant was an instant hit with celebrities, business leaders, and tourists from all over the world. In the elegant dining room, guests pay from $100 to $400 Singaporean dollars (around $300 U.S.) for full meals.

[5] A few of the selections on the menu are quite exotic. Deep-fried scorpions with stingers still attached are recommended to soothe the nerves and cure migraine headaches. For rheumatism, try "Ants Climbing up the Tree," a "tree" of potato and lettuce with fried black ants. Such dishes may not appeal to everyone, but most items on the menu are Chinese dishes made with herbs, vegetables, seafood, and meat. Try it—you'll like it!

Imperial Herbal Restaurant, 3rd Floor Metropole Hotel, 41 Seah Street, Singapore 188396, telephone: 337-0491

4. *Write the **topic** of each paragraph here. Were your predictions correct?*

[1] _____ *Introduction* _____

[2] _____

[3] _____

[4] _____

[5] _____

5. *Is there anything else you would like to know that is not in the review?*

_____

6. *Find words or expressions in "Bugs Part of the Cure" with similar meanings to the words listed here. In the reading, underline the words or expressions—**the context clues**—that gave you the answer.*

ANSWER KEY

Paragraph 2

a. doctor _____

b. someone who prepares and
sells medicine _____

c. the cook _____

Paragraph 4

d. sudden success _____

Paragraph 5

e. choices _____

f. unusual _____

7. *Complete the sentences with one of these words or expressions from the reading.*

ANSWER KEY

prescribe   approach to   attract attention   medical check-up

certified   sound like   soothe the nerves

A restaurant that serves scorpions for dinner is sure to

_____. The Imperial Herbal Restaurant, with its
      (a)

unusual _____ food and health did just that
        (b)

when it opened in Singapore. Eating dinner there can be some-

what like having a _____ with Li Lian Xing, a
        (c)

_____ pharmacist strolling among the diners.
    (d)

Dr. Li may _____ a special dish to
        (e)

_____ or a certain kind of diet to give you more
   (f)

energy. This restaurant may not _____ your cup
        (g)

of tea, but it has been very successful so far.

8. *Some of the words in the selection may be unfamiliar to you because they are unusual terms. Can you identify which unfamiliar words are probably related to food and which are related to health? Make a list here. Then compare your list with a classmate's.*

Related to Food

_____

_____

_____

_____

_____

_____

Related to Health

_____

_____

_____

_____

_____

_____

Quickwriting: Favorite Restaurants

Think about your favorite restaurant. Why is it your favorite? Is it the food? The atmosphere? The view? The service? In your notebook, write for five to ten minutes about this topic.

Reading 2

Cheap Eats

People are always interested in good restaurants that are also inexpensive.

1. *Skim the short restaurant reviews that follow. Which restaurant sounds most interesting to you? Write the name here. Then read "Cheap Eats."*

_____

Cheap Eats

Thai Delight

People who like spicy food will be delighted with Thai Delight, a new restaurant in the Central District. Located in the building previously occupied by a drugstore, the restaurant has no atmosphere to speak of, but the prices make up for this lack and you can expect friendly service. The Pad Thai, a traditional noodle dish that usually includes shrimp, didn't have any shrimp, but costs only $3.85 at lunch time. I recommend the chicken with basil and the Masaman curry. Both were cooked to perfection and were served with rice and a small salad with peanut dressing. This restaurant is a great find for people who want good food at affordable prices.

Thai Delight, 18756 Jackson Street. Open from 11:00 a.m. to 2:00 p.m. and 5:00 p.m. to 10:00 p.m.

Polynesian Hut

The Polynesian Hut couldn't be located in a more convenient place —right in the heart of the business district. However, location is probably the only thing this restaurant has going for it. It's almost too dark to see the decor of plastic tropical plants and thatched "huts." The menu includes such items as sweet and sour shrimp (tastes a lot like ketchup), a very mushy chicken with cashew nuts, and barbecued pork (actually quite good). Prices range from $4 to $7.50 for lunch and $6 to $10 for dinner. Since everything is prepared (long) ahead of time, this is a good place to eat if you are in a hurry and hungry! The servings are very large.

Polynesian Hut, 4th and Broadway. Hours: Daily 11 a.m. to 11 p.m. All-you-can-eat buffet on Saturdays from 11 to 3.

International Deli

Are you looking for a fast, affordable place for lunch? The International Deli may fit the bill. Although not truly international, the selection in this deli is quite varied, including French baguettes with a selection of meats and cheese, Chinese pot stickers and hum bao, Scottish meat pies, and sushi. I highly recommend the Indonesian rice salad and the teriyaki chicken wings. Prices are reasonable, ranging from $2 to $5. Seating is limited, but the deli is clean and bright with large windows and lots of interesting souvenirs on the walls from the owners' travels.

International Deli, 6175 Walnut Street. Open for lunch only, 10:30 to 3:00, Monday through Friday.

Whistle Stop Café

You won't hear any train whistles, but the new café in the old train station takes full advantage of the location. Photos on the walls illustrate the history of the railroad, from the first trains to modern-day monorails, and the long, narrow room with a counter opposite the cooking area reminds diners of being on a train. The food is certainly not standard train fare, however. The chef and owner, Marco Lott, cooks a variety of homestyle soups, fresh salads, and delicious sandwiches, all served on homemade bread. Try the papaya chicken salad ($4.50) or the turkey sandwich with apple chutney ($3.95). The desserts are worth a special trip, especially the cheesecake and the fruit tart.

Whistle Stop Café, King Street Station. Open Daily 6:30 a.m. to 10:00 p.m.

2. *Which restaurant did you choose in exercise 1?* **Write notes** *here about information you would like to remember if you decide to try this restaurant. Reread the review of that restaurant, if necessary.*

_____

_____

_____

_____

3. *Discuss your choice with a classmate. Why did you like that restaurant best? Compare your notes, too. Do you both have all the information you would need about the restaurant?*

4. *Food reviews contain lots of adjectives to give readers a clear picture of the food, the service, the decor, and the prices of an eating establishment. With a partner, reread "Cheap Eats" to complete the middle column of this table. Then brainstorm some other appropriate adjectives and complete the last column for a food review. Share your results with the rest of the class.*

	Adjectives from "Cheap Eats"	*Brainstormed Adjectives*
Ten adjectives that describe food		
Five adjectives that describe decor or atmosphere		
Two adjectives that describe cost		
Two adjectives that describe service		

Targeting

Expressions for Reviews and Recommendations

Certain words and expressions are commonly used when you write a review or a recommendation.

1. *Study the words and expressions on page 77.*

Expressions Related to Restaurants	Examples
be **located** [*somewhere*]	The restaurant is **located** near the market.
menu **includes** [*something*]	Its menu **includes** items from a lot of countries.
[*collection of things*] **including** [*something*]	Its menu has a variety of desserts **including** flan and a delicious strawberry cheesecake.
have/make/offer/serve [*something*]	They **offer** something for every taste. They **serve** a lot of pasta dishes. They **make** the best cheesecake in town.
[*something*] **costs** [*amount*]/**between** [*one amount*] **and** [*another amount*]	All the entrees **cost between** $10 **and** $15. Nothing **costs** more than $10.
The **cost of** [*something*] **is** [*high/low/average*] **compared to/with** this [*something else*]	The **cost** of a meal at the Tower **is** average **compared with** other restaurants that offer this kind of view.

Expressions Related to Recommendations	Examples
recommend [*noun*]	I don't **recommend** the Polynesian Hut to anyone concerned about cleanliness.
recommend that [*someone*] [*base form of the verb*]	I **recommend that** you try the barbecued beef.
The **best/worst thing about** [*something*] **is** [*noun*]	The **best thing about** the Pizza Express **is** its convenient location.
The **best/worst thing about** [*something*] **is** [*how/where/that . . . subject, verb*]	The **best thing about** the Pizza Express **is** where it is located. The **worst thing about** this restaurant **is** how slow the service is.

2. *Write sentences to describe a restaurant you know. Use the words in parentheses.*

  a. (is located) ———————————————————————.

  b. (offers) ———————————————————————.

  c. (include) ———————————————————————.

  d. (including) ———————————————————————.

  e. (cost) ———————————————————————.

  f. (recommend that) ———————————————————————.

  g. (the best thing) ———————————————————————.

···

When you give your opinion about a place, it always helps to give details.

1. *You are going to write a review of a restaurant, cafeteria, or coffee shop for your local newspaper. What kind of information is usually included in a review?*

_____   _____

_____   _____

_____   _____

_____   _____

2. *Think of some eating places near you, including restaurants that you like and a few that you don't like. List them here.*

_____   _____

_____   _____

_____   _____

3. *What kind of specific information would someone want to know about these places? Write notes about each place here.*

Restaurant 1	Restaurant 2	Restaurant 3

Writing a Review

Write reviews of two different places to eat. Don't limit yourself to restaurants. Take a look at other places to eat, such as snack bars, coffee stands, or campus cafeterias. Use some words and expressions from the chart in Targeting Expressions for Reviews and Recommendations on pages 77–78. If necessary, go to the restaurants to find out specific information that your reader might want to know.

Editing and Rewriting

Editing for Colons and Semicolons

The use of colons and semicolons can be tricky. This section provides an overview of the uses of these two punctuation marks.

1. *Study this information about the use of colons and semicolons.*

Rules for Colon Use	*Examples*
A colon comes at the end of an independent clause. It introduces a list or additional information.	This café serves specialty coffee drinks: espressos, cappuccinos, and lattes. The notice on the wall is very clear: Please do not occupy the table for more than one hour.
Don't use a colon immediately after a verb, preposition, or expression like *such as* or *for example*.	*Incorrect* The items on the menu are: spaghetti, penne, and ravioli. I am hungry for: Chinese, Mexican, or Thai food tonight. It has a variety of pasta dishes such as: spaghetti, penne, and ravioli.

Rules for Semicolon Use	Examples
Semicolons are often used to connect two independent clauses. However, the ideas in the two clauses need to be closely related. Often, the second clause explains the first clause in different words.	The restaurant is very reasonable; nothing on the menu costs more than $6. The service is terrible there; we waited an hour for our dinner to be served by a rude waitress!
Semicolons are used with transitional expressions that show cause-result, addition, or contrast. Notice in the examples that the transitional expressions are followed by a comma.	They have terrible service at that restaurant; as a result, we won't go there again. *(cause-result)* They brought all of the chopped ingredients to the table; then they stir-fried them in front of us. *(addition)* The restaurant is expensive; however, the price is worth it. *(contrast)*
Semicolons also separate items in a list when there is a comma in one of the items.	The menu includes some regional favorites: red beans and rice; shrimp, fish, and crab gumbo; and turtle soup.

2. *Put a check (✓) in front of the sentence(s) with correct punctuation.*

ANSWER KEY

a. _____ The restaurant offered a variety of desserts: including cheesecake, pie, and ice cream.

b. _____ People with a low tolerance for spicy food should not try the chicken soup: it brought tears to my eyes.

c. _____ The restaurant got good recommendations when it

opened, however, the quality seems to have deterio-
rated over time.

d. _____ I would highly recommend all three restaurants:
Chutney's, Raga, and the Maharaja.

e. _____ The service is slow; in fact, it was so slow that we missed
the movie we had planned to go to.

f. _____ I recommend this restaurant highly; it is sure to be a
success!

g. _____ We sampled three of the appetizers: smoked salmon;
marinated asparagus tips; and coconut shrimp, served
with an excellent sauce for dipping.

h. _____ Their famous desserts are: mud pie (an ice cream dish
that tastes better than it sounds), almond mocha torte,
and pears with caramel sauce

Editing Checklist

Check the Content

1. *Exchange your restaurant reviews with a classmate. After you read your class-mate's reviews, answer these questions:*

   ❑ Is it clear to you whether the reviewer liked the restaurant or not? Are
   there enough examples or reasons that the restaurant is good or bad?
   ❑ Is there any additional information you would like to know about either
   restaurant?

Check the Details

2. *Now, reread your own reviews. If necessary, revise them. Add more details or clar-ify information. Then continue checking your own writing. Use these suggestions:*

   ❑ Reread "Cheap Eats" on page 75 and the words and expressions related to
   restaurants and recommendations on pages 77–78. Did you use any of the
   same expressions from these sources in your reviews? Check to see if those
   expressions are correct.
   ❑ Check the subject and verb in each sentence for verb agreement and tense.
   ❑ Check for correct use of colons and semicolons, especially in any lists.

3. *Revise your writing.*

Vocabulary Log

What words or phrases would you like to remember from this chapter? Write five to ten items in your notebook. Examples are on page 12.

Grammar and Punctuation Review

Look over your writing from this chapter. What changes did you need to make in grammar and punctuation? Write them in your notebook. Review them before the next writing assignment.

Class Activity   Restaurants

1 What kind of restaurant do you wish you had in your area? Design the perfect restaurant. Write a proposal in which you consider location, menu choices, cost, atmosphere, and any other relevant topics. Share your ideas with your classmates.

OR

2 Make a newsletter with reviews of places to eat near your school. Include information about atmosphere, clientele, and eating customs that a newcomer to the area would like to know about.

③ Musical Notes

The appeal of music is universal, but different styles of music appeal to different people. This unit explores several topics related to music. These are some of the activities you will do in this unit:

- Read notices of concerts
- Read about research on the benefits of music
- Discuss and write about your musical experiences
- Read part of a directory of musical instruments
- Write technical definitions
- Read about the development of a style of music in the United States
- Write a description related to music

Chapter 7

In Concert

An interest in music can start early and continue throughout your life. In this chapter you will read concert announcements and a report on the benefits of music. Then you will write about your own experiences with music.

Starting Point

What kind of music do you like?

Musical Tastes

1. *Look at these photographs. Discuss the questions with a partner or a small group.*

   a. What kind of music are these performers playing?

   classical music   rock   folk music   country music   jazz

b. How do you feel about music? What kind of music do you like?

Reading 1

What's Happening

(ANSWER KEY)

Newspapers usually list musical events in the entertainment section.

1. *Scan the concert listings. Circle the type of music in each concert.*

 What's Happening

TODAY:

Dar Williams – 8 p.m. Folk singer/songwriter performs at Meany Hall. Tickets $15. 528-8523.

Chansonnier – 7:30 p.m. Musical group Chansonnier performs medieval pieces including songs of the Troubadours. Free. McKinley Hall's E.E. Bach Theatre, Pacific University. 281-2959.

Carmen – Western Opera Theatre performs Bizet's work at the Performing Arts Center tonight at 8 p.m. Tickets $30. 2710 Wetmore Ave. 257-8888.

Tucker Martine – 8 p.m. Progressive jazz trio performs at Earshot Jazz Festival. Poncho Concert Hall, Cornish College. Tickets $10-$12. 547-9787.

The Refreshments – 7:30 p.m. Rock band The Refreshments performs with opening act Artificial Joy Club at RKCNDY, 1812 Yale. Tickets $7. 628-0888.

Hank Williams Jr., Travis Tritt, and Charlie Daniels – 5:30 p.m. Country artists perform at the Dome. Tickets $25. 628-0888.

Aerosmith – 8 p.m. Veteran rock band Aerosmith performs at Key Arena. Tickets $25-$35. 628-0888.

SUNDAY:

Dance Hall Crashers, MXPX – 7 p.m. Rock bands Dance Hall Crashers and MXPX perform at DV8, 131 Taylor Ave. Tickets $10. 628-0888.

The Marriage of Figaro – The University School of Music performs Mozart's work in its Seattle Opera Preview series. 1:30 p.m. Free. Brechemin Auditorium. 685-8384.

Diane Schuur – 7 p.m. and 9:30 p.m. Jazz singer Diane Schuur performs with her trio at the Performing Arts Center, 2710 Wetmore Ave. Tickets $26. 257-8888.

Baroque Orchestra – 8 p.m. Violinist David Greenberg joins the orchestra in performing 'Folias' by Vivaldi and Germinani with other works by Corelli, D. Scarlatti, Pergolesi, and Rossi. Tickets $12-$20. St. Stephen's Episcopal Church, 4805 45th Street N.E. 325-7066.

Music in the Park – 2:30 p.m. The Northwest Chamber Orchestra performs classical works by Franz Joseph and Michael Haydn. Tickets $12.50; children 17 and under free with paying adult. Asian Art Museum, Volunteer Park. 343-0445.

2. *Which concert would you be most likely to attend? Write the information you would need to know in order to get to the performance.*

TO DO
☐ Check with S. about concert
☐
☐

3. *Scan the listings again. Answer these questions:*

ANSWER KEY

   a. Which event is the most expensive? _____

   b. Which is the least expensive? _____

   c. What information does each listing provide? _____

   _____

....

Many people enjoy listening to music, but few realize how beneficial this activity can be, even at a very early age.

1. *Read the selection on the next page.*

Reading 2

Benefits from Music

READING TIP

When you read an article that gives an opinion, think about whether you agree or disagree with the writer. As you read, analyze the support that the writer gives.

[1] The students at a class at Texas Christian University may seem a bit unusual. They are only 4 to 11 months old, but they are students in "Musical Beginnings," a course for parents and infants. Classes such as this are becoming increasingly popular among parents.

[2] How early should music be a part of children's lives? It's never too early, according to studies. Lorna Zemke, a professor of music, advocates playing music during pregnancy. She believes that children who hear music before they are born have "advanced skills in socialization, verbalization, and overall alertness." Researchers at Brigham Young University found that premature babies who listened to classical music "gained more weight, cried less, were healthier, and left the hospital an average of three days earlier than those not exposed to classical music."

[3] In a study reported in the journal *Neurological Research,* researchers divided preschoolers into three groups. One group took piano lessons, another took computer lessons, and a third group received neither. The children who took piano lessons scored 34% higher on tests than the others. The researchers concluded that piano instruction increases children's abstract reasoning ability, a skill essential for math and science. They are continuing to study the relationship between early music lessons and developmental changes in the brain.

[4] Research with older children also points to the benefits of music instruction that go beyond test results. Students gain self-esteem and learn the value of lessons when they go from knowing nothing about an instrument to being able to play it. They learn self-discipline and time management as they take lessons and practice. In a musical group, they learn the value of teamwork.

[5] Not every child will grow up to be a composer like Mozart, a violinist like Midori, or a guitarist like the late rock guitarist Jimi Hendrix. However, the enjoyment and benefits of musical education appear to extend beyond virtuosos.

2. *Writers often use pronouns or demonstrative adjectives to* **refer** *to nouns mentioned before. What do the underlined words in each item refer to? Look in the reading.*

   a. [1] <u>They</u> are only 4 to 11 months old. _____

   b. [1] Classes such as <u>this</u> are becoming increasingly popular.

   _____

   c. [2] Premature babies who listened to classical music "gained more weight, cried less, were healthier, and left the hospital an average of three days earlier than <u>those</u> not exposed to classical music."

   _____

   d. [3] One group took piano lessons, <u>another</u> took computer lessons, and a third group received <u>neither</u>.

   _____

   e. [3] The children who took piano lessons scored 34% higher on tests than the <u>others</u>.

   _____

   f. [3] <u>They</u> are continuing to study the relationship.

   _____

   g. [4] In a musical group, <u>they</u> learn the value of teamwork.

   _____

   h. [4] Students gain self-esteem and learn the value of lessons when they go from knowing nothing about an instrument to being able to play <u>it</u>.

   _____

3. *The author of "Benefits from Music" feels that music is good for young people. Complete these exercises to determine how well the author supports her thesis.*

    a. In this chart, **take notes** from the reading. Put a check mark (✓) to identify the type of support used.

Support	Age Group	Type of Support	
"Musical Beginnings"	4–11 months (infants)	Research Opinion Activity	❑ ❑ ☑
Lorna Zemke		Research Opinion Activity	❑ ❑ ❑
Brigham Young University		Research Opinion Activity	❑ ❑ ❑
	preschoolers	Research Opinion Activity	❑ ❑ ❑
	older children	Research Opinion Activity	❑ ❑ ❑

    b. Look at your notes in the chart. **Analyze the support** the writer gives.

        1. Which support do you think is the strongest? _____

        2. Which is not supported as well? _____

        3. The researchers at Brigham Young University used classical music in their study. The writer does not give information about why the researchers chose classical music instead of other types. What are some reasons that you can think of?

        _____

4. Researchers have also shown that listening to classical music before an intelligence test improves scores. Why do you think this would be true?

_____

5. What is your opinion? Does a teenager in a neighborhood rock band benefit as much as a teenager in the high school band?

_____

4. *Some friends of yours have mentioned in a letter that they are thinking about giving their three-year-old daughter lessons in music or gymnastics. Write them a quick note, **summarizing** what you have read in "Benefits from Music" and giving your opinion. Do NOT look back in the reading.*

_____

_____

_____

_____

_____

_____

5. *Go back to the reading. Underline the words and phrases that the writer uses to refer to other people's opinions or research. Compare the formal style of the reading with your informal summary in exercise 4 above.*

··

Targeting

Word Forms

If you know common endings for different word forms, you can improve your reading.

1. *Complete the chart on the next page with the missing **word forms**.*

(ANSWER KEY)

Verb	Noun	Adjective
	socialization	
	verbalization	
	alertness	
	researcher	
	reasoning	
		essential
	relationship	
instruct		
		developmental
	management	
		musical
	composer	
	enjoyment	
	education	

2. *Underline any consistent endings you see in the chart for verbs, nouns, and adjectives. Write them here.*

Verb endings   _____

Noun endings   _____

Adjective endings _____

3. *Complete these sentences with one of the words from the chart in exercise 1.*

a. When Andrew was young, he didn't really like interacting with

other children. He wasn't very _____ . Playing

in the school band helped him learn to _____ .

b. I don't understand her _____ . Why did she

decide to stop playing the piano when she was so good at it?

c. The violin is _____ to the cello. They are both string instruments.

d. Drums are _____ to most music because they give the rhythm.

e. None of us had any formal music _____ . We all learned to play on our own.

f. Taking music lessons helps young people to _____ self-discipline.

g. Beethoven became deaf as he grew older, but he continued to _____ music.

h. The concert was very _____ . I can't remember another concert I _____ this much!

i. They were well _____ in most areas, but they never studied music.

How important is music in your life? In your notebook, write for five to ten minutes on this topic.

··

1. *Draw a timeline in your notebook. Indicate the following on your timeline.*

your earliest memories of music

music you heard in your home

the kinds of music you have liked at various times in your life

singing experiences

experiences playing an instrument

concert experiences

Quickwriting: Music

Writing

Preparing to Write: Using a Timeline

2. *Look again at your timeline. Circle the entries that are most significant in your relationship with music.*

Writing a Personal Narrative

Write about music and you—your experiences or feelings about music. Use your notes from Preparing to Write.

Editing and Rewriting

....

Editing Checklist

Check the Content

1. *Exchange your narrative with a classmate. After you read your classmate's narrative, answer these questions:*

   ❑ Can you understand the writer's main ideas?
   ❑ Are there enough details to support his or her main ideas?

Check the Details

2. *Read your own narrative again. If necessary, revise what you wrote. Add or change details. Then continue checking your own writing. Use these questions:*

   ❑ Check the subject and verb in each sentence for verb agreement and tense.
   ❑ Check pronouns and demonstrative adjectives for correct reference.
   ❑ Are all the sentences complete?

3. *Revise your writing.*

Vocabulary Log

What words or phrases would you like to remember from this chapter? Write five to ten items in your notebook. Examples are on page 12.

Grammar and Punctuation Review

Look over your writing from this chapter. What changes did you need to make in grammar and punctuation? Write them in your notebook. Review them before the next writing assignment.

Chapter 8

The Musician's Tools

Starting Point

The topic of music provides a good opportunity for working on some technical skills. In this chapter you will read descriptions of musical instruments and write definitions.

Traditional Instruments

Traditional musical instruments illustrate the uniqueness of cultures around the world.

1. *Look at these traditional instruments from around the world. Can you name them?*

2. *What instruments have you and your classmates studied?*

Reading

Directory of Musical Instruments

A directory is an easy reference for information about instruments.

1. ***Predict*** *what information the directory will give about each instrument.*

2. *Read the descriptions of musical instruments. Were your predictions correct?*

Directory of Musical Instruments

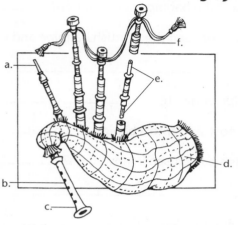

Bagpipe

The bagpipe is a musical instrument that was most common in European countries during the Renaissance. It is still common in folk music in Europe and in military music in Britain. The bagpipe has reed pipes that work when air is moved from an attached windbag. In the old days, these bags were made from a whole skin of a small animal, but now they are made with pieces of leather or synthetic materials. The piper plays the melody on the chanter, the pipe with fingerholes. The other pipes are called drones. Scottish bagpipers blow into a tube connected to the bag. French bagpipes, called the musette, get air from bellows that the player moves with his or her arm. The origin of the bagpipe is not known.

Banjo

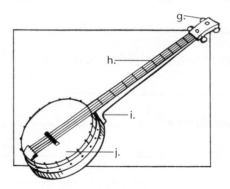

The banjo is a string instrument with a circular resonating box (usually a hollow wooden case) attached to a long neck. The strings extend from below the sound box to the top of the neck. They are tightened with thumb screws. To play the banjo, you press the fingers of one hand at different places on the strings along the neck while you strum or pluck the strings over the resonating box. The banjo developed from the West African long-necked lute (a pear-shaped, plucked instrument dating back at least 2,000 years). It came to the United States with the slave trade and was a common instrument for early African-American music. In the early twentieth century, the banjo became an important rhythmic instrument of the jazz band. It is still a common instrument in bluegrass and some other forms of country music.

Drum

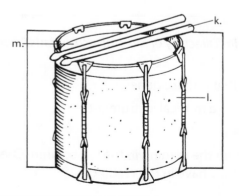

A drum is a percussion instrument made by stretching a skin or other material over one or both ends of a hollow container. Drummers strike the head of the drum either with the palm of the hand or with some type of stick. Although drums are most often used to accompany other instruments, music made by drums alone plays an important ceremonial or religious role in many cultures. Historically, drums have also been used to communicate from one group of people to another far away.

ANSWER KEY

ANSWER KEY

3. *Label the illustrations with terms from the reading. Example:*
   a. blowpipe.

4. *Answer the questions about the reading.*

   a. When was the bagpipe most popular? _____

   b. In what kind of music is the bagpipe still common? _____

   c. What is the difference between the Scottish bagpipe and the

   French musette? _____

   d. Where did the bagpipe originate? _____

   e. What instrument is most similar to a banjo? _____

   f. What kind of music is a banjo used in nowadays? _____

   _____

   g. How do you play a banjo? _____

   _____

   h. How did the banjo come to the United States? _____

   _____

   i. How do you make sounds on a drum? _____

   _____

   j. What role have drums played in societies around the world?

   _____

ANSWER KEY

5. *Analyze the vocabulary* in "Directory of Musical Instruments." Complete these tasks.

   a. Circle the expression that is more general.

   a string instrument   a musical instrument

   a percussion instrument

   b. Look at the phrases from the reading in the left column. Check
   (✓) the function that they have in the reading.

Phrases	Gives information about the history or typical use	Shows how the instrument works	Shows the materials or structure of the instruments
was common during	✓		
work when air is moved from . . .			
in the old days			
has reed pipes			
were made from a whole skin of an animal/with . . .			
The origin of the . . .			
. . . instrument with a circular box attached			
To play the . . . , you press the fingers of one hand at different places on the strings while you . . .			
The . . . developed from the . . .			
drummers strike the . . . with a . . .			
. . . are most often used to . . .			
Historically . . .			

Writing

Preparing to Write: Analyzing Parts of Definitions

Every field has terminology that not everyone may understand. Writers explain such terms in a technical definition. A technical definition has three parts: the term, its category, and what makes it different.

term   **category**   **what makes it different**

A bagpipe is a *musical instrument* that *was popular during the Renaissance.*

term   **category**   **what makes it different**

The banjo is a *string instrument* with *a circular resonating box attached to a long neck.*

1. *Write **T** (term), **C** (category), and **D** (difference) above the parts of each definition.*

   a. Electronic music is music that is generated or reproduced electronically.

   b. A synthesizer is an electronic musical instrument that is used to generate or control electronic sounds.

   c. The clavichord is a string instrument with keys developed in the fourteenth century.

   d. The bagpipe drones are pipes that make a continuous low sound.

   e. The musette is a French bagpipe that has bellows instead of an air tube.

   f. The balalaika is a Russian instrument with a triangular body that has a flat back and a slightly curved front.

   g. The dombra is an instrument in the guitar family that predates the balalaika.

2. *Write definitions for these terms.*

	term	category	difference
a.	composer	a person	writes music

A composer is a person who writes music.

	term	category	difference
b.	musician	a person	plays music
c.	piano	a keyboard instrument	hammers that strike wire strings
d.	musical arranger	a person	adapts a musical composition to a particular style of performance or instruments
e.	reggae	a type of music	a particular beat which originated in Jamaica

Think of the different kinds of music that you are interested in. Write definitions for the kind of music, instruments, or any technical terms.

Writing Technical Definitions

Editing and Rewriting

Editing for Adjective Clause and "Of" and "For" Phrase Errors

· ·

Be careful with adjective clauses and "of" and "for" phrases when you write definitions.

1. *Read the rules on the next page for writing sentences with adjective clauses or "of" and "for" phrases.*

Rules	Examples
Make sure the subject and verb agree when you use an adjective clause.	Violin and piano are *instruments* **that require** a lot of practice. Playing in a marching band is *an activity* **that keeps** you fit.
Use **who** or **that** for people to connect an adjective clause to the main clause. Use **which** or **that** for things unless the adjective clause gives additional information. In that case, use **which** and a comma to separate the information from the rest of the sentence.	She's the woman **who (that)** composed that song. The Autoharp™ is an instrument **that** requires a lot of practice. For Princess Diana's funeral, Elton John rewrote *A Candle in the Wind*, **which** he had originally written to remember Marilyn Monroe. NOT: For Princess Diana's funeral, Elton John rewrote *A Candle in the Wind*, **that** he had originally written to remember Marilyn Monroe.
Make sure that **of** and **for** are followed by gerunds (verb + *ing*), not the simple form of the verb.	Regular practice is a requirement **of (for) learning** an instrument. Plucking is a technique **of sounding** the strings on an instrument.

2. *Correct the errors in these sentences.*

a. Line dancing is an activity which are growing in popularity.

b. The neck is the place on the instrument that having the strings.

c. The school orchestra is an organization which have fewer members than the marching band.

d. Plucking is a method of pull and release the strings on an instrument.

e. Music is an activity who brings people closer together.

f. The conductor is the person who lead the orchestra.

g. Amplification is a way of make sound louder.

Editing Checklist

Check the Content

1. *Exchange your definitions with a classmate. After you read them, answer this question:*

   ❏ Does every definition have a term, a category, and information about how it is different?

Check the Details

2. *If necessary, revise your definitions. Then continue checking your own writing. Use these questions:*

   ❏ Do the subjects and verbs agree in the adjective clauses?
   ❏ Do **of** or **for** phrases have a gerund (verb + *ing*) or a noun phrase in them?

3. *Rewrite your technical definitions.*

Vocabulary Log

What words or phrases would you like to remember from this chapter? Write five to ten items in your notebook. Examples are on page 12.

Chapter 9

All That Jazz

Rock and jazz are music styles of the twentieth century, so we know a lot about their history. In this chapter you will read about jazz and write about a musical style of your choice.

Starting Point

What Do You Know?

Jazz swings in and out of popularity with the general public. How do you feel about this musical style?

Discuss these questions with a partner or a small group:

a. Are you familiar with any of these jazz musicians or singers?

Louis Armstrong	Stan Getz	John Coltrane
Ella Fitzgerald	Joao Gilberto	Chick Corea
Wynton Marsalis	Sun Ra	Kenny G.

b. Do you like to listen to jazz? Why or why not? Which kind(s) of jazz do you prefer?

Jazz: A Break from Tradition

Jazzy, jazzed up, and *all that jazz.* It's not just a type of music. The influence of jazz even extends to our everyday speech. This reading will give you information about jazz.

1. *Based on the title of the reading, how do you expect this information to be organized?* **Predict** *what the organization of this selection will be.*

   _____

2. *Now skim the first sentence of each paragraph in the reading. Were you correct in your prediction?*

3. *Read the following selection.*

Jazz: A Break from Tradition

[1] Although jazz is now played in concert halls around the world, the beginnings of jazz were closely tied to the community and the African-American experience. Like the city of New Orleans where it began in the early 1900s, jazz is a mixture of Euro-American and African influences. Early jazz combined the original instruments and harmony of the Euro-American tradition with African rhythm, drums, and an emphasis on improvisation (making new melodies as you play).

[2] The earliest jazz was not a collection of written music, but rather a style of playing among black musicians in small musical combos and marching bands in New Orleans. These musicians "jazzed up" traditional songs by changing the rhythm and improvising. Brass instruments (trumpets, trombones, and clarinets) played the melody, and drums, bass, or piano made up the rhythm section. A string instrument like the guitar or banjo was also typical in early jazz. As musicians from New Orleans traveled to New York and Chicago in the 1920s and 1930s, jazz quickly caught on with the American public. Louis Armstrong was one of the most well-known jazz musicians at this time and is considered to have influenced all the musicians who followed him.

[3]   As jazz bands grew larger, more musical arrangements were written down. The improvisation was left to solo performers such as Billie Holiday and Lester Young. New York took over from New Orleans as the center of jazz. This period was known as the Swing or Big Band era when jazz was extremely popular for both listening and dancing. Band leaders like Duke Ellington and Benny Goodman became well-known to the American public.

[4]   The "bebop" style of jazz developed in the 1940s as a reaction to the carefully orchestrated "swing" music of the mainstream big bands, popular in the 1930s and 1940s. Smaller jazz combos featured solo jazz musicians such as Charlie Parker, Dizzy Gillespie, and Thelonius Monk playing trumpet, saxophone, or piano. "Bebop" or "bop" was not for everyone. Its fast and unusual harmonies and rhythm were not easy to dance to, and this kind of jazz did not catch on with the general public.

[5]   Jazz has always alternated between periods of having an established "mainstream" musical style and periods of rebellion against that established style. This was certainly true in the period between 1950 and 1980. In the 1950s, as a reaction to the extremes of "bebop," "cool" jazz became popular. Miles Davis was one of the most prominent performers of that era. "Cool" jazz featured less improvisation and a smoother, slower sound with instruments such as the flute and the French horn. Then once again, jazz musicians rejected too much regularity and returned to improvisation. The "free jazz" of the 1960s featured artists such as Cecil Taylor and John Coltrane who played dissonant and atonal music. In the early 1970s, musicians such as Herbie Hancock, Miles Davis, and Chick Corea played heavily amplified jazz using electric guitars and keyboards.

[6]   Through the years, jazz has become popular around the world and has, in its turn, been influenced by the music of other countries, Latin American and African in particular. Current jazz is an international mix of both contemporary and traditional sounds. With its tradition of improvisation and independent musicians, jazz will never stay the same for long.

4. *Write a* **topic** *outline of the selection.*

Jazz

[1] _____Introduction_____

[2] _____

[3] _____

[4] _____

[5] _____

[6] _____

5. *Read each pair of sentences. Which sentence in each pair is specific? Which is general? Write* **S** *or* **G** *on the blank lines.*

a. __S__ Jazz began in New Orleans.

_____ Jazz has become popular around the world.

b. _____ Jazz alternated between periods of having an established musical style and periods of rebellion against that established style.

_____ The "bebop" style of jazz developed in the 1940s as a reaction to the carefully orchestrated music of the big bands.

c. _____ Charlie Parker became well-known during the "bebop" era.

_____ The "bebop" style of jazz developed in the 1940s as a reaction to the carefully orchestrated music of the big bands.

d. _____ Jazz is a mixture of many different styles and musical traditions.

_____ Through the 1930s and 1940s, the big bands played "swing" music, popular for dancing.

e. _____ Improvisation is a key feature of jazz.

_____ During the "swing" era, the improvisation was left to solo performers such as Billie Holiday and Lester Young.

f. _____ The banjo was used in early jazz.

_____ Many of the early instruments of jazz were instruments from marching bands.

g. _____ Improvisation was left to solo performers.

_____ For example, Lester Young was a famous jazz soloist.

h. _____ Jazz has changed over the years.

_____ Although it started in the United States, jazz is now international.

i. _____ "Bebop" was not as popular with the general public as "swing."

_____ Jazz became very popular.

6. *If you know common endings for different **word forms,** you can improve your reading. Choose one of the words in parentheses to complete the sentences.*

a. Contemporary jazz is a _____ (mixture, mixed) of many different musical influences.

b. When musicians improvise, the music doesn't sound very

_____ (harmony, harmonize, harmonious). However, they usually come back to play the

_____ (harmony, harmonize, harmonious) at the end.

c. Jazz has always had a strong _____ (emphasis, emphasize) on improvisation.

d. What kind of _____ (music, musical, musician) influences have changed the current sound of jazz?

e. Experienced _____ (music, musical,

musicians) usually love to _____

(improvise, improvisation).

f. I know the song, but I have never heard this

_____ (arrange, arranger, arrangement).

g. My favorite is _____ (tradition, traditional)

jazz.

h. How did the public _____ (react, reaction)

to the new sounds?

i. In the 1970s, musicians started to _____

(amplify, amplification) their instruments.

....

Reading 2

The Songsters

In this age of international concert tours and CD releases, it doesn't take long for artists to become famous everywhere.

1. *Look at the following list of people in the music world. Choose one of them to read about.*

Whitney Houston, a vocalist

Elton John, a singer, songwriter, and pianist

Garth Brooks, a country music singer and songwriter

Bob Marley, a reggae musician and songwriter

2. *Find and read the short selection on page 110 about the person you chose (only that person!). As you read, **take notes** on the timeline.*

The Songsters

Whitney Houston

Whitney Houston was born in New Jersey in 1963. Her mother, Cissy Houston, was a singer, and her cousin was a famous pop singer, Dionne Warwick. When she was 22, Houston recorded her first album. Houston is known for the wide range of both her voice and her repertoire. In 1993, Houston began acting in movies, starring with Kevin Costner in "The Bodyguard" and, in 1995, starring in "Waiting to Exhale."

Elton John

Elton Hercules John was actually named Reginald Kenneth Dwight when he was born in 1947. A singer, pianist, and composer, John (along with lyricist Bernie Taupin) had his first success in 1970 with two albums, "Elton John" and "Tumbleweed Connection." Between 1972 and 1975, he had seven albums that reached number one on the charts, one right after the other. Elton John was as well known for his fanciful costumes and elaborate stage performances as for his music. In 1975, he sang "Pinball Wizard" in "Tommy," a rock opera. John continued to record albums through the 1990s and was very active in AIDS research and charity. In 1997, he gained the public's attention once more when he sang a new version of his composition "Candle in the Wind," a song originally written about Marilyn Monroe, at the funeral of his friend Princess Diana.

Garth Brooks

Garth Brooks was born in Oklahoma in 1962. Brooks grew up listening to rock music. He became a country music singer, but the rhythm and topics of his music came from rock. On his first album in 1989, he had four number one songs on the country charts, and in 1991, "Ropin' the Wind" became a huge "crossover" success with country, pop music, and rock audiences. Brooks's music was largely responsible for the popularity of country music with the general public in the 1990s. Brooks is one of the most popular performers in the United States. In 1990, tickets for 18,000 seats in one arena were sold in 37 minutes! In 1994, Brooks decided to stop touring in order to spend more time with his family, but he continues to record new songs.

Bob Marley

Bob Marley was born in Jamaica in 1945. With his group, the Wailers (formed in 1964), Marley brought reggae, a style of music with its roots in the poorest areas of Kingston, to international popularity in the 1970s. Their music, which included such popular songs as "I Shot the Sheriff" (1973) and "Rastaman Vibration" (1976), influenced many songwriters around the world, both because of the unusual reggae rhythm and because of its political statements. Although reggae lost some of its popularity after Marley's death in 1981, his son, Ziggy Marley, produced successful reggae albums, and the reggae influence is clear in the "rap" music of the 1980s and 1990s.

3. *Talk to a classmate who read about a different person. Exchange information by* **summarizing** *the information from the reading in your own words. Refer back to your notes on the timeline, if necessary.*

Targeting

Transitions

Transition expressions help make your writing clear.

1. *Study the information about transitions on page 112.*

Rules	Examples
Transition expressions usually occur at the beginning of a sentence, or independent clause, followed by a comma.	A studio recorded their music. **However,** they never produced a CD. Banjos were common in jazz until the 1930s. **After that,** they weren't.
Coordinate conjunctions also connect ideas. They join two sentences and require a comma before them.	The band had a CD out**, but** it didn't bring in enough money for them to give up their jobs. I like classical music**, so** I usually buy season's tickets to the symphony.
Subordinate conjunctions connect dependent clauses to main clauses. When the dependent clause comes at the beginning of the sentence, it is followed by a comma.	**Because** she was so popular, it was hard to get tickets to her concerts. It was hard to get tickets to her concerts **because** she was so popular. NOT: It was hard to get tickets to her concerts, **because** she was so popular.
Prepositions may have the same meanings as subordinate conjunctions, but they are followed by a noun phrase rather than by a clause.	Tickets to her concerts were hard to get **because** she was so popular. *(subordinate conjunction followed by a clause)* Tickets to her concerts were hard to get **because of** her popularity. *(prepositional phrase "because of" followed by a noun phrase)*

2. *Complete the sentences with expressions from this list. You may use the expressions more than once.*

because   but   because of this
however   so   for example

Contemporary music sometimes contains things that parents object to. ___*For example*___ , rock music often
(a)
uses objectionable language. Rap music also offends parents

_____ it sometimes talks about violence and
(b)

abuse. _____ , parents' groups in the United
(c)

States have worked to try to make changes in the music

industry. _____ , they have forced music com-
(d)

panies to label CDs and music videos that have objectionable

content. Music companies have agreed to these restrictions,

_____ many people call this unnecessary.
(e)

They think that parents should be more active in monitoring

their children rather than relying on labels to restrict their

access to objectionable music.

3. *Connect these ideas. Use the words in parentheses.*

a. I like rock music. I never go to concerts. They are too loud.
(however, because)

_____

b. The amplifiers at rock concerts make the music extremely loud. Doctors warn people about potential damage to their ears. *(for this reason)*

_____

c. Many people who are middle-aged now grew up listening to loud rock music. They need hearing aids. *(because)*

d. Doctors recommend that you be careful when you go to rock concerts. They recommend putting cotton in your ears. *(for example)*

e. Most young people don't want to look different from their peers. They aren't likely to wear cotton in their ears. *(so)*

Writing

Preparing to Write 1: Mapping

When you are trying to decide what to write about, **mapping in a diagram** can help you develop your ideas.

1. *Think of two musical styles. Write them in the following circles.*

   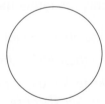

2. *What information comes to mind when you think of these styles? Are there any issues or interesting people connected to these musical styles? Add any names, dates, or other bits of information on lines around the circles to collect your ideas.*

3. *Look at your mapping diagrams again. Circle or highlight the information you think would be most interesting to write about.*

4. *Your assignment is to write about a musical style, about an issue in contemporary music, or about a famous person in the music field. Do you want to write about one of the music styles/people/issues or more than one? Plan your writing here.*

    a. What is the main idea that you want to say? Write an introductory sentence.

    b. Make a topic outline to help you organize your writing.

Although some writing is primarily one style (time order, cause and effect, comparison and contrast), most writing is a combination of several styles. You can use many different kinds of support to explain your main ideas. The following exercises show some examples of different kinds of support.

Preparing to Write 2: Organizing Support

1. *Read the description of jazz. What kind of information is the writer giving? Choose from the list. There may be more than one kind in each section.*

Cause/effect   Definition   Comparison/contrast   Time order

a. _____

_____

The first jazz musicians played in African-American marching bands that often led funeral processions to the cemetery. On the way to the cemetery, they played traditional hymns. On the way back, they played "jazzed up" versions of the same hymns. The first recordings of jazz music were made in 1917.

b. _____

_____

Early jazz was more of a style of playing than a collection of written music. The musicians in small jazz bands did not write down a certain way to play a song. When jazz became more mainstream, however, the bands became larger and the songs were written down. Improvisation, always a component of jazz, was left to solo performers.

c. _____

_____

Big band leaders such as Fletcher Henderson played a style that was known as "swing." Like other forms of jazz, swing music featured call and response, a style in which one section of the band played followed by a "response" from another section.

d. _____

_____

"Bebop" or "bop" was a reaction to the big band era of jazz. Bop musicians didn't like the restrictions of music that was written down and played the same way over and over again. Therefore, they returned to the original, small combo style of playing, with its focus on improvisation. This change also reflected the social and political changes of the "Beatnik" era and a return to the African-American roots of jazz.

e. _____ Instead of a consistent, harmonious
_____ sound that was easy to listen to, bop
was very complex. No one could dance
to it because, unlike swing, bop had no
consistent rhythm. Bop was a turning
point from the old traditions of dance-
able music to modern jazz, in which
music is considered an art form.

f. _____ Preservation Hall was opened in New
_____ Orleans in 1961. At Preservation Hall,
musicians play traditional, early jazz
songs such as "When the Saints Go
Marching In." This emphasis on tradition
was in sharp contrast to the develop-
ments in jazz at the time. In 1960,
Ornette Coleman's "Free Jazz" album
featured eight musicians, all improvising
without any harmonic themes at all.
John Coltrane continued the exploration
of alternative jazz through the 1960s
with wild, atonal instrumentation.

2. _Use ideas from your mapping diagram in Preparing to Write 1 and
write your own examples of each style of information._

   a. Cause/effect

   _____

   _____

   b. Comparison/contrast

   _____

   _____

   c. Definition

   _____

   _____

   d. Time order

   _____

   _____

Writing a Description

Use your notes from Preparing to Write 1 on pages 114–115 to write about a musical style, an issue in contemporary music, or a famous person in the music field.

Editing and Rewriting

Editing for Punctuation with Subordinating Conjunctions and Adverbial Expressions

When you combine ideas or include transitions in your writing, the punctuation is sometimes tricky.

1. *Study these rules.*

Rules	*Examples*
When two clauses are connected with a **subordinating conjunction,** a comma is not necessary.	They still had office jobs **when** they started to play together.
If the **subordinating conjunction** and dependent clause are at the beginning, you need a comma after the clause.	**When** they started to play together, they still had office jobs. **Because** the band was so new, they played in small bars and music clubs.
Adverbial expressions at the beginning of a sentence or independent clause are separated from the rest of the sentence with a comma.	**Finally,** they made enough money through their music to support themselves. **At that point,** they were able to quit their other jobs.

For more information about transition expressions, see Reference, pages 246–248.

2. *Put a check (✓) in front of the sentence(s) with correct punctuation.*

ANSWER KEY

a. _____ In the 1920s and 1930s, country music was associated mainly with people from the mountains of the South.

b. _____ They sang songs influenced by English, Irish, and Scottish folk tunes of the 1600s, however the music was also influenced by African-American music.

c. _____ When cowboy music started to influence country music it became known as country and western music.

d. _____ For example there were several famous singing cowboys, Roy Rogers and Gene Autry.

e. _____ By the 1950s, country and western music was no longer popular only in the South.

f. _____ Country and western music was once popular only in the rural South and Southwest of the United States. Now, however, it is popular all over the country.

g. _____ Some people called the music "country rock" when musicians started to use electric instruments in the 1970s.

Editing Checklist
Check the Content

1. *Exchange your description with a classmate. After you read your classmate's work, answer these questions:*

   ❑ Do you understand the main ideas?
   ❑ Does the writer provide enough support for the ideas?

Check the Details

2. *Read your own writing again. If necessary, revise. Add or change details. Then continue checking your paper. Use these questions:*

   ❑ Check the subject and verb in each sentence for verb agreement and tense.
   ❑ Are all the sentences complete?
   ❑ Check for transitions and conjunctions in your writing. Is the punctuation correct?

3. *Revise your writing.*

Vocabulary Log

What words or phrases would you like to remember from this chapter? Write five to ten items in your notebook. Examples are on page 12.

Grammar and Punctuation Review

Look over your writing from this chapter. What changes did you need to make in grammar and punctuation? Write them in your notebook. Review them before the next writing assignment.

Class Activity   The Music Scene

Choose one activity:

1 Research places in your area to listen to music. Which places would you recommend to others? Prepare an information sheet or poster with your recommendations. Post or distribute it where newcomers to your program will be able to read it.

2 Choose a musical event from your local newspaper. Go to the event with some of your classmates. After the event, tell your classmates about it, in either a written review or a conversation.

3 The musical history of jazz is only half the story. This period of history was also a time of many changes in race relations in the United States. Music is important in almost every political, religious, or social movement. Choose a kind of music or a song that reflects a broader change. Bring in a song, photos, or a poster to illustrate and explain the significance.

4 The Games We Play

Playing games is a popular activity in many cultures. In this unit, you will read and write about a variety of games.

Here are some of the activities you will do in this unit:

- Read and write about a childhood game
- Read about what makes games successful
- Write a summary
- Design a game and write game directions

Chapter 10

It's How You Play the Game

This chapter gives you practice in reading and writing game descriptions.

Starting Point

To Begin Play

Although there are many different games in the world, there are common rules for playing them.

1. *With a classmate, write these game expressions under the correct picture.*

a deck of cards	the person who is "it"	necessary objects
playing pieces	the winner and the loser	roll the dice

a.

b.

c.   d.   e.

f.

2. *Think of games you played as a child. Write the names of some games here and discuss them with a classmate.*

a board or tile game: _____

a physical skill game: _____

a fantasy (make-believe) game: _____

a card game: _____

Reading

Kick the Can

Remember the games you played as a child with the neighborhood children? Here's a variation on a universal childhood game of tag.

1. *Read the following selection.*

Kick the Can

[1]   When I was growing up, the children in my neighborhood had a lot of fun playing games together outside in good weather. In late spring, when the days were getting longer, we finished our homework quickly so that we could get outside for a couple of hours of games in daylight. During the summer vacation months, we played all afternoon, ate dinner fast, and went outside again until dark. The games we chose depended on how many children were around that day. There were tag games and fantasy games, but the most popular game on our block was Kick the Can, which is a variation of Hide and Seek.

[2]   In the version of Kick the Can that I played, you need at least six children, a yard with hiding places, and an empty tin can. The person who is "it" puts her foot on the can, covers her eyes, and counts to 100. In that time everyone else runs and hides. The person who is "it" then looks for the other children. If she sees someone, for example, "David," she runs back and jumps over the can shouting, "Over the can for David!" Then David has to come in and stay in the area designated as the "jail." As the person who is "it" finds more and more people, the jail gets fuller. However, the exciting part of the game is that at any time, a person can run in while the person who is "it" is out searching for people. The runner kicks the can as far as possible, yelling, "Kick the can!" This action sets everyone in "jail" free, and they run quickly to hide again. The person who is "it" has to retrieve the can and start all over again, covering her eyes and counting to 100 again. The game is over when everyone is in "jail." The first person to be put in "jail" is the person to be "it" in the next round of the game.

[3]   This game has only a couple of special rules. First, you can hide only in one yard and the boundaries have to be very clear. Second, in some neighborhoods, the players allow the people in "jail" to give clues to hiders about when it is safe to come in and kick the can. However, on our block we considered that cheating.

[4] Although I don't see children playing games outside much any-
more, in the warm months, when I smell cut grass, I remember my
mother calling me to come in for bed and how hard it was to leave a
game of Kick the Can.

2. **Take notes** from the reading "Kick the Can" to complete this chart.

ANSWER KEY

Description	Examples
What you need	
How to begin the game	
	"Over the can for (. . .)!"
When the person who is "it" may have to begin the game again	
Special rules	
When the game is over	

READING TIP

Taking notes in a chart from a reading can help you under-stand the ideas in the reading better.

3. *Circle the letter of the statement that is NOT true about "Kick the Can."*

ANSWER KEY

   a. You need daylight to play this game.

   b. This game is similar to Hide and Seek.

   c. In the author's neighborhood, you could give hints to hiders about when it was safe to kick the can.

   d. Captured children could be set free if someone kicked the can.

Do you have memories of playing with children in your neighborhood? In your notebook, write for five to ten minutes on this topic.

Quickwriting: Games

Targeting

....

Game Expressions

Think of games that you used to play. Use the bold-faced expressions to write sentences about games you know.

1. ***We always played this game*** *at birthday parties.*

   We always played this game at Grandma's house because she

   let us climb her tree.

2. ***You need*** *at least six people* ***to play this game.***

   _____

3. ***The object of the game is to*** *capture the other team's flag.*

   _____

4. ***In order to win this game,*** *you have to go around all five holes successfully.*

   _____

5. ***One of the reasons I really like this game is*** *that in a very short time you know who the winner is.*

   _____

6. ***The difficult part of this game was*** *that you had to run a lot and I was never a good runner.*

   _____

Writing

Preparing to Write 1: Narrowing a Topic

After you choose a topic to write about, you need to narrow it with specific details.

Think about a game you enjoyed playing in your childhood. Check (✓) all of the following that are true for your game.

a. This game is

    _____ a fantasy game.

    _____ a physical skill game.

    _____ a board or tile game.

    _____ a card game.

    _____ a guessing or luck game.

b. It requires

    _____ objects or equipment.

    _____ more than two players.

    _____ mental skills.

    _____ luck.

c. It is

    _____ a very old traditional game.

    _____ not played much by children today.

d. The winner

    _____ has the most (money, tokens, points, cards) at the end of the game.

    _____ is the first person to _____.

Preparing to Write 2: Organizing Information

1. *In the chart are some typical sentences from game descriptions. The list contains topic headings for the descriptions. Write the topic headings above the correct descriptions.*

Conclusion

How to Play the Game

✓ Introduction

How to Begin Playing

What You Need

Penalties or Special Rules

The Object of the Game

How to Determine the Winner

a.	Introduction	b.	
	No one knows exactly <u>when this game started</u>, but it has been a tradition in my country for many years. We have a lot of <u>special games for</u> New Year's Day.		To play this game, you need a small soft ball and a triangular-shaped roof. You don't need any special skills to play this game, so it works with children of different ages.
c.		d.	
	We did rock-scissors-paper to decide who was "it." We flipped a coin to determine which team would begin first.		The object of the game is to capture the other team's flag.
e.		f.	
	After that, the player has to grab the handkerchief and run after the child who dropped it. Then you throw the sticks high up into the air and shout how you hope they will land.		If you missed catching the ball, you had to stand against the wall. Then everyone was entitled to hit you with their balls. This was a terrible penalty! This game is very simple, but we made it more interesting by having funny penalties. For example, the person had to say the alphabet backwards.

g.	**h.**
If one person in team B breaks through team A's lines, his or her team wins. The last player who has the most fingers unfolded is the winner.	Once when we were playing this game in the attic in the dark, my brother fell and hurt himself. After that, we were never allowed to play this game inside again. These days it is very quiet in the alley behind our house because all of the children have grown up, and they no longer play this game.

2. *Look at the sentences in exercise 1 again. Underline key expressions that would be useful in any game description. The first one is done for you.*

3. *Some of these sample sentences are in the present tense and some are in the simple past tense. Why? Discuss your answers with a partner.*

Writing a Process Description

Now write a composition about a game from your childhood. In a logical order, describe the game and how to play it. Include a beginning, a middle, and an end. Refer to the Organizing Information exercises in Preparing to Write 2 for ideas about order. Reread that section and Targeting Game Expressions for useful expressions.

Editing and Rewriting

Editing for Articles and Nouns in Generalizations

It's important to learn correct article use with nouns when you make generalizations.

1. *Read these rules and examples.*

Rules	Examples
There are two common ways to make generalizations with count nouns. Use the indefinite article (**a, an**) with the singular noun or make the noun plural. The sentences on the right have the same meaning.	**A board game** can be very educational. **Board games** can be very educational.
Don't use indefinite articles with noncount nouns.	**Milk** is good for your body. **Money** can't buy love. NOT: According to **a research**, . . .

For more information about noncount nouns and plural nouns, see Reference, page 244.

2. *In your writing, remember to think about articles when you decide whether to use a singular or a plural noun in a generalization. In the following sentences, put an X by all of the sentences with errors in generalizations. Then correct them. You may need to add or delete an article, or you may need to make a noun singular or plural.*

ANSWER KEY

a. _____ Charades is game that is usually played indoors.

b. _____ The only equipment you need is pencil and small piece of paper.

c. _____ Then divide into team.

d. _____ It helps to choose captain for each team, but it's not necessary.

e. _____ Teams go to separate rooms so that they cannot hear each other.

f. _____ Each team decides on names of famous person, movies, and books.

g. _____ You must have one name for each member of the other team.

h. _____ When the teams come back together in one room, each team takes turns.

i. _____ Each player gets slip of paper.

j. _____ They can use only actions to get their team to guess the name.

k. _____ If teammate can guess the name, that team gets a point.

l. _____ Charades is an easy and fun game to play with a small number of rules to follow.

m. _____ First, the player who is doing the acting cannot make any sound.

n. _____ Second, he or she may point to person in the room, but he may not use object in the room.

o. _____ Another rule is that player may use action or gesture but cannot spell out word with hand.

p. _____ It's okay for teammate to talk and ask question.

q. _____ The team that took the least amount of time is the winner.

Editing Checklist

Check the Content

1. *Exchange your process description with a classmate. After you read your class-mate's description, answer these questions:*

    ❏ Is there a clear sense of a beginning, middle, and an end to the description?
    ❏ Is the object or goal of the game clearly explained?
    ❏ Is the "how to play" section arranged in the order the game is played?
    ❏ Are there enough transition words *(first, next, finally)* to make the steps clear?

Check the Details

2. *Now, reread your description. If necessary, add or clarify information. Then continue checking your own writing. Use these questions:*

    ❏ Did you put events that happened in the past in the past tense?
    ❏ Are the instructions for playing the game in the present tense?
    ❏ Do subjects and verbs agree?

3. *Revise your writing.*

Vocabulary Log

What words or phrases would you like to remember from this chapter? Write five to ten items in your notebook. Examples are on page 12.

Grammar and Punctuation Review

Look over your writing from this chapter. What changes did you need to make in grammar and punctuation? Write them in your notebook. Review them before the next writing assignment.

Chapter 11

Ahead of the Game

Starting Point

In this chapter you will read about what makes games successful and you will write a summary of an article.

Board Games

Although there are hundreds of board games around the world, most of them fall into these categories:

- race games—who can get there first (for example, Parcheesi™)
- war games—who can acquire the most (for example, Monopoly)
- position games (for example, chess)
- solving the puzzle games—who was the murderer? (for example, Clue)

1. *Do you know these games? Work with a partner to identify them. What are they called in your language?*

2. *Discuss these questions with a classmate. Then report your ideas to the class.*

  a. What is the most popular board game among adults in your country?

  b. What is the most popular board game among children?

  c. Do teenagers like to play board games? Which ones?

  d. What must game manufacturers consider when they are designing a game for the international market?

  e. What do you think is the most popular board game around the world?

Reading 1

The Games Nations Play

What makes a game successful across cultures? There is a lot to consider in order to design a game that has universal appeal.

1. *Read the following article by Michael Tate and Martin Croft to find out which games have universal appeal.*

The Games Nations Play

[1] Games that are successful in one country do not always sell well in another. A good example is the question game called Trivial Pursuit. This game became an instant hit in the United States and in Great Britain in the early 1980s. In Trivial Pursuit, players move their markers around a board and answer questions in categories, such as Entertainment or Sports. Although Waddington Games, the company that sells the game, made a lot of money, it was a failure in Japan. According to the head of the company in London, people in Japan were embarrassed to "lose face" when they got an answer wrong. This is a good example of how game makers must consider cultural differences when they market a product abroad.

[2] An example of a successful cross-cultural game is Monopoly. In this board game, developed during the Great Depression of the 1930s, players make "money" from buying and selling property, building houses and hotels, and charging other players rent. Monopoly is the world's favorite board game, with annual sales of 450,000 sets in Britain alone, nearly equal to one game per house-

hold. Monopoly has even bigger sales in the United States and is now produced in twenty-five languages, including Russian, Croatian, and Hebrew. Interestingly enough, Monopoly was not allowed in the old Soviet Union because it is a capitalistic game, emphasizing private ownership of property, rather than government ownership. For the same reason, it is not played in the People's Republic of China. However, six sets were taken to an exhibition in Moscow in 1959, and all six disappeared during the exhibition. Today, when it is easy to sell Monopoly in Russia, the American and British English versions sell much better there than the Russian language version.

[3] In Germany and Austria, history has played a role in games. Game manufacturers have agreed never to make board games that show violence (no explosives or guns) or make references to Nazi Germany. Some German game companies have tried to create "cooperative" board games with no competition of any sort among the players, or games where everyone can win. Despite these limitations, Germany is the world's biggest game-playing nation, and Germans prefer lots of detail and many rules. According to Roger Heyworth, marketing director of Gibson Games, "Germany is a much bigger market, certainly in terms of games that make you think." For example, one British game, Fair Means or Foul, sold only 15,000 copies in Britain, but its German version sold 500,000 copies at a price 50 percent higher than the British version.

[4] Another complication when selling games overseas is translating a language that has thousands of characters, such as Chinese or Japanese, into a tile game, such as Scrabble. In Scrabble, players must work with seven tiles at a time to build words on the game board. The words must connect as they would in a crossword puzzle. Scrabble is now published in thirty-one languages, including Slovak, Greek, and Arabic. However, it hasn't been published in Mandarin Chinese. A Japanese version is in the works. This version uses a kind of shorthand Japanese that people in business prefer. In the meantime, the Japanese play the English language versions with Japanese rule books.

[5] The problem market for game companies within Britain is the late teens and early 20s group. Mature adults buy board games, but young people are less interested. With the introduction of games on CD-ROM and on the Internet, manufacturers hope to sell games to

many more young people. Monopoly and Trivial Pursuit are already on CD-ROM and are being played on the Internet. Risk, a war strategy game with visually exciting features, will soon be available. Clue, a detective, murder mystery game, and Battleship, a naval warfare game, are in the making. It is possible that no matter where young people live in the world, they will be attracted to the technology of these games.

2. *In the context of this reading, how are these words related? Write the* **topic** *on the line below each set of words.*

    a. buying and selling   building houses   charging rent
        property   and hotels

                        actions in Monopoly

    b. Trivial Pursuit   Monopoly   Scrabble   Risk   Clue

    c. Waddington Games   Gibson Games

    d. explosives   guns   reference to Nazi Germany

    e. Monopoly   Trivial Pursuit   Risk   Clue   Battleship

    f. solving a   answering questions   building words
        murder   in categories   with tiles

        making money   engaging in
        from owning   naval warfare
        property

    g. Slovak   Greek   Arabic

3. *The reading gives specific examples to support general statements. What are these words and phrases examples of? Write the general **topic** next to the specific example.*

ANSWER KEY

a. Entertainment or Sports   *categories in Trivial Pursuit*

b. losing face   _____

c. Chinese   _____

d. Trivial Pursuit   _____

e. Monopoly   _____

4. *In English, each paragraph focuses on one topic. What the writer has to say about the topic is the main idea. Circle the number of the best **main idea** sentence for each paragraph.*

ANSWER KEY

a. Paragraph 1
  1. Trivial Pursuit was not a hit all over the world.
  2. Trivial Pursuit was not successful in Japan.
  3. Games may sell well in one country and be a failure in another.
  4. Some games are too embarrassing in some cultures.

b. Paragraph 2
  1. Monopoly is a good example of how some games are not popular in some cultures.
  2. Monopoly is the most popular game all over the world.
  3. Monopoly is successful only in Communist countries.
  4. Monopoly is a game about buying and selling property.

c. Paragraph 3
  1. Germany is a big market for games.
  2. History can affect the kinds of games that are popular in a country.
  3. Germans like to play games that are complex but nonviolent.
  4. One British game was more successful in Germany than in Britain.

d. Paragraph 4

1. The Japanese have to play Scrabble with an English version.
2. To play Scrabble, you must make words out of seven tiles.
3. Scrabble is popular in many parts of the world.
4. It is hard to translate games into languages that are based on characters rather than alphabets.

e. Paragraph 5

1. The new technology of games played on computers will attract young people around the world.
2. The problem market for game companies within Britain is the late teens and early 20s group.
3. Mature adults are more interested in board games than young people are.
4. Manufacturers are producing games on CD-ROM and on the Internet.

Reflect on Reading

You found the **main idea** in exercise 4. The main idea is the most important thing the writer says about the topic. It may or may not be directly stated. It is the general idea that covers all of the details in the paragraph or reading.

In which of these situations would finding the main idea be important? Discuss with a partner or a small group.

| Reading directions for a game | Reading a textbook for a course | Reading a novel |

Reading 2

Non-Game Games

The games people play tell us a lot about the social life of a culture.

1. *Read the following selection by Lena Williams.*

Non-Game Games

[1] Adult Americans are spending their free time at home playing games at a pace not seen since the 1950s when television was just beginning to be a means of home entertainment. Thirty years ago games were seen as child's play. Today they are viewed as entertainment and perfectly acceptable for adults to play. The games adults

---

READING TIP

Don't worry about words that are unfamiliar to you. Just keep reading for the general meaning.

seem to enjoy the most are those that play down the need to win. One expert calls these less competitive games "non-game games."

[2] According to John F. Kelly, a writer and games collector, the games we play usually show what is going on in society's mind. "In the eighteenth century, there were a lot of explorer and travel games. In the '30s, people wanted to turn their lives around: boy makes good." That's when Monopoly became popular. Some of the games on the market now show that Americans are definitely not in a serious state of mind. Games that take more than three minutes to explain, that take hours to play, or that require a player's undivided attention are unlikely to sell nowadays. According to Jonathan Bard of Stoler & Bard, the public-relations company that represents the makers of the top-selling Pictionary, a sort of charades played on paper, today's games are "attractive on the outside, easy to understand."

[3] Dr. Angelo S. Longo, a game developer, believes that people are playing games for social reasons. People come away from a game experience with a feeling that it was fun, rather than a feeling of winning or losing. "Games provide a safe structure in which people can socialize," said Dr. Sherri MacIngo, a professor at the University of Southern California, whose specialty is demographics. Dr. MacIngo believes games give people a chance to express their hidden emotions. She knows people whose personalities change almost totally when they play games. The good thing is that people don't need to apologize or make excuses for their changed behavior because they are in a game-playing atmosphere.

[4] Toy analysts believe the renewed interest in adult games is due not only to a longing for the past but also to a need for escape from a fast-paced, stressful world. "Basically, we're all out of control in the work environment," said Dr. Longo. "When you play a game, the structure of the game gives you control." Because players understand the rules and the limits, Dr. Longo feels that games give people confidence in themselves.

[5] Although the majority of Americans still spend most of their leisure time watching television, there appears to be growing interest in activities that contrast with watching television and that may be causing a new interest in games. Some worry that the mindlessness

of many games indicates Americans are losing their competitive instincts. However, there is no need to worry about this. According to Dr. Longo, we haven't lost the sense of competition. We have just gained more pleasure in playing.

2. *Answer these questions about "Non-Game Games.":*

   a. What is the different view of games today versus the view thirty years ago?

   _____

   _____

   b. What kinds of games are the most popular?

   _____

   _____

   c. What do some of today's games tell us about American society?

   _____

   _____

   d. According to Dr. Longo, what is more important in today's games: to win or to enjoy yourself?

   _____

   _____

   e. Why are games considered a safe way for people to socialize?

   _____

   _____

f. What contrast does Dr. Longo make between working and playing a game?

_____

_____

g. Does Dr. Longo think that Americans are losing their competitive edge?

_____

_____

3. *Practice the vocabulary in the reading. In pairs, discuss the following questions using the expressions in italics from the reading.*

a. Do you have a strong *sense of competition*?

b. Does your *personality* change when you play games?

c. What are some *adult games* that people play in your culture?

d. What do you usually do in your *leisure time*?

e. Do you have a *growing interest in* anything at present?

f. What is the best *work environment* for you?

g. What is your favorite form of *entertainment*?

h. What do you consider to be a *mindless* activity?

Targeting

The Language of Summaries

A summary is a short version of an original writing. It's important to know how to report the author's ideas and sometimes the author's words in a summary. However, using someone else's writing as if it were your own is called plagiarism. Always avoid plagiarism in your writing. Whenever possible, restate the author's ideas in your own words and indicate whose ideas you are rephrasing. If you want to use the author's words, you must put them in quotation marks (" . . . ").

1. *Keep these points in mind when writing a summary.*

Guidelines	Examples
Begin your summary with a phrase to introduce the source.	**According to** Lena Williams, . . . **In** Lena Williams's **article** "Non-Game Games," . . .
Use reporting verbs to express the author's ideas.	The author **argues / claims / states / believes / suggests / maintains / discusses / presents / gives** . . .
Some reporting verbs take an object. However, most reporting verbs are followed by a noun clause.	The author discusses/presents **the results of three studies**. *(object)* The author argues/suggests **that competitive games are less important than they used to be.** *(noun clause)*
In a long summary, you will need to refer to the author from time to time so the reader will know these are still the author's ideas, not yours.	The author **further/also** states . . .
You can also use transition expressions that show you are still summarizing.	**Furthermore/In addition** . . . **Moreover,** the author believes that . . .

2. *Complete the following sentences, using the language of summaries.*

a. _____ Tate and Croft's _____, " _____

_____," the authors

discuss the factors that influence a game's success.

b. _____, they present the problem of

making games attractive to young people.

c. _____ Tate and Croft, a game that is

popular in one country may not be a success in another.

d. Tate and Croft _____ claim that character

languages complicate the cross-cultural success of word

games.

e. The authors _____ an example of the

game Monopoly.

f. The authors _____ that consumers in

their late teens or early 20s are a problem market.

g. _____, the authors explain the difficulties

in translating certain languages into tile games.

· ·

Writing

The steps in this section will help you write a summary, your next
writing task.

The first step in writing a summary is to find the most important elements, or the main ideas. In exercise 4 on pages 137–138, you circled
the sentences that expressed the most important elements of "The
Games Nations Play."

**Preparing to
Write 1: Steps for
Writing a Summary**

1. *Look at your choices on pages 137–138 again. Which paragraph's main idea would also work for the whole reading? Write this main idea here.*

_____

_____

2. *The second step in writing a summary is to consider the best way to introduce the other main ideas. It is important to tell the readers who the author of the article is in the introduction. Which sentence would be a good way to introduce the main idea of "The Games Nations Play" for a summary? Circle the letter.*

   a. Tate and Croft wrote an article about the games different countries like to play. They state that . . .

   b. In their article, "The Games Nations Play," Tate and Croft state that . . .

   c. The article by Tate and Croft says that . . .

3. *Combine the introduction you just chose with the main idea of the article in exercise 1 to begin a summary of "The Games Nations Play."*

_____

_____

4. *If you've already introduced the article and its authors, you may need to make a second reference to the authors of the article. Which sentence would be a good way to refer to the authors the second time when summarizing their ideas? Circle the letter.*

   a. The authors also state that . . .

   b. In "The Games Nations Play," the authors . . .

   c. In their article "The Games Nations Play," Tate and Croft state that . . .

5. *Combine the best sentence in exercise 4 with another idea in the article to write a reference to the authors in your summary.*

_____

_____

Follow these steps to prepare to write a summary of Reading 2, "Non-Game Games," on pages 138–140.

1. *What is the main idea of each paragraph?*

Paragraph 1 _____

_____

Paragraph 2 _____

_____

Paragraph 3 _____

_____

Paragraph 4 _____

_____

Paragraph 5 _____

_____

2. *What is the main idea of the whole reading? Use your own words to state it.*

_____

_____

3. *How will you begin the summary? Write an introduction.*

_____

_____

4. *Will you refer a second time to the author? If so, write the reference sentence with additional information from the article.*

_____

_____

Writing a Summary

WRITING TIP

Add transition words to make your ideas connect smoothly.

Now you are ready to write a summary of "Non-Game Games."

Use your answers in Preparing to Write 2 and vocabulary from Targeting the Language of Summaries to write a summary of the main ideas in "Non-Game Games."

Editing and Rewriting

Editing for Errors with Count Nouns

Count nouns are nouns that can be singular or plural: **a** friend, **two** friend**s**, **this** book, my English book**s**. A common mistake is to forget the plural **-s** or **-es** for count nouns. When you are editing, look at every noun and decide if it should be plural.

1. *Study this information.*

Rules	*Examples*
A count noun can never be bare or stand alone.	*INCORRECT* There are cat here. I have cat. It's cat. Where is cat? We gave cat a name.
This means the count noun must be "covered" by a plural ending or a determiner. A determiner gives information about a noun. Typical determiners are articles, possessives, demonstratives, and quantifiers.	*CORRECT* *Add a plural ending:* There are cat**s** here. *Add a determiner:* I have **a** cat. *(article)* It's **my** cat. *(possessive)* Where is **that** cat? *(demonstrative)* We gave **each** cat a name. *(quantifier)*

Rules	Examples
Adjectives give **extra** information about nouns, but they are not determiners.	*INCORRECT:* They are beautiful cat. *CORRECT:* They are beautiful cat**s**.
If you have a bare count noun in your writing, something is wrong. Ask yourself: 1. What can I add to "cover" this noun? 2. Is the noun really plural? (Add a plural ending.) 3. If the noun is really singular, can I add a determiner? Which determiner?	*INCORRECT* *CORRECT* We are friend.→ We are friend**s**. I have friend.→ I have **a** friend. He's friend.——→ He's **my** friend.

For information about plural nouns, see Reference, page 245.

2. *Check every noun in the sentences on page 148. Underline the bare, singular count nouns. Circle words that signal that a plural form should be used. Decide if the noun needs a plural form, such as **-s** or **-es**, and add it. Some sentences may be correct.*

ANSWER KEY

Putting Fun Back on Board

EDITING TIP

Reading aloud may help you hear where the plural endings are missing.

(a) While playing game is a typical activity of childhood, youngster today typically play with electronic games. **(b)** These games are very different from the traditional board games their parents may have played. **(c)** According to Carol Seefeldt, a professor of human development at the University of Maryland, board game are better because they help develop thinking skills. **(d)** Seefeldt also believes that child are basically self-centered. **(e)** They do not realize that other people may not share all of their idea. **(f)** Traditional game help them learn that their own way of thinking is not the only way. **(g)** Board games develop math and reading skill, as well as social and basic life skills, like how to win or lose graciously, says Stevanne Auerbach, a California psychologist and former consultant for a large game company. **(h)** Children also learn how to play fairly, take turn, follow direction, concentrate until something is finished, and stay with a project without the necessity for rapid graphics. **(i)** In contrast, electronic games establish expectation of an entertaining and fast-paced life. Auerbach maintains that a child needs to learn that not everything in life happens quickly.

(j) Some person feel electronic games also develop cognitive skill or require specialized knowledge. **(k)** Karen Peck, a spokeswoman for Nintendo Entertainment Systems, says Nintendo games help child develop their ability to get information from several sources at once. **(l)** Some people praise these games because they give feedback and levels of complexity. **(m)** However, critic feel that video and computer games are inferior because children effectively play alone.

(n) How can parents pull child away from electronic games to play an old-fashioned board games? **(o)** Simple. There is nothing more satisfying to children than to have time with parent. **(p)** Schedule some game-playing time into family time. Make it exciting; for example, play by candlelight, use flashlight, play specific music. **(q)** Offer a choice; keep a variety of games in the home. **(r)** Invite friends and relative to join in the fun.

Editing Checklist

Check the Content
1. *Exchange your summary with a classmate. After you read your classmate's summary, answer these questions:*

   ❏ Does the summary begin with an introduction of the author and the name of the reading?
   ❏ Are all of the main ideas included?
   ❏ Is the author referred to later in the summary?

Check the Details
2. *Now, reread your summary. If necessary, revise it. Add or clarify information. Then continue checking your own writing. Use these questions:*

   ❏ Do transition words connect the main ideas?
   ❏ Did you use correct articles and nouns to make generalizations?
   ❏ If any singular count nouns are bare, fix them.

3. *Revise your writing.*

Vocabulary Log

What words or phrases would you like to remember from this chapter? Write five to ten items in your notebook. Examples are on page 12.

Grammar and Punctuation Review

Look over your writing from this chapter. What changes did you need to make in grammar and punctuation? Write them in your notebook. Review them before the next writing assignment.

Chapter 12

If You
Pass Go,
Collect $200.

Clear directions are important to the success of any game. This chapter gives you practice with reading and writing technical directions.

Starting Point

Ready? Set?

Monopoly, a game of buying and selling property, is the most popular board game around the world.

The picture shows the equipment necessary to play Monopoly. Draw lines from the terms in the list to the game parts.

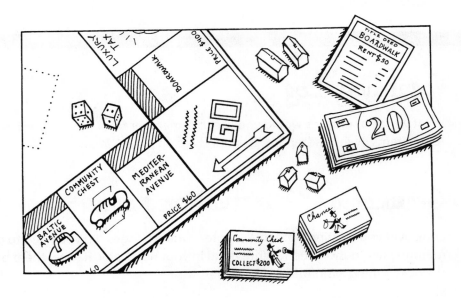

a. game pieces

b. houses

c. hotels

d. Chance and Community Chest cards

e. a title deed

f. play money

g. dice

h. game board

Monopoly

Before you play a game, it is important to read the directions. Most directions have sections with headings. Under these headings, you can expect to find certain information.

1. *Look at the list of headings in the second column. They are from the directions for Monopoly in the reading that follows. Under which heading would you expect to find the phrases in the third column? Write the number of the phrase next to the heading.*

Number	Heading	Phrase
_____	**a.** Object	**1.** When you land on property owned by another player . . .
_____	**b.** Equipment	**2.** Each player is given . . .
_____	**c.** Preparation	**3.** . . . to become the wealthiest player . . .
_____	**d.** The Play	**4.** . . . consists of a board, 2 dice . . .
_____	**e.** Paying Rent	**5.** Starting with the Banker, each player in turn throws the dice . . .

2. *Read these game directions for playing Monopoly.*

Monopoly

Object

The object of the game is to become the wealthiest player through buying, renting, and selling property.

Equipment

The equipment consists of a board, 2 dice, tokens, 32 houses, and 12 hotels. There are Chance and Community Chest cards, a Title Deed card for each property, and play money.

Preparation

Place the board on a table and put the Chance and Community Chest cards face-down on their allotted spaces on the board. Each player chooses one token to represent him/her while traveling around the board.

Each player is given $1500 divided as follows: 2 each of $500's, $100's, and $50's; 6 $20's; 5 each of $10's, $5's, and $1's. All remaining money and other equipment go to the Bank.

Banker

A banker who plays in the game must keep his/her personal funds separate from those of the Bank.

The Play

Starting with the Banker, each player in turn throws the dice. The player with the highest number starts the play. Place your token on the corner marked "GO," throw the dice, and move your token in the direction of the arrow the number of spaces indicated by the dice. After you have completed your play, the turn passes to the left.

According to the space your token reaches, you may be entitled to buy real estate or other properties or obliged to pay rent, pay taxes, draw a Chance or Community Chest card, "Go to Jail," etc.

"Go"

Each time a player's token lands on or passes over "GO," whether by throwing the dice or drawing a card, the Banker pays him/her a $200 salary.

Buying Property

Whenever you land on an unowned property, you may buy that property from the Bank at its printed price. You receive the Title Deed card showing ownership; place it face up in front of you.

Paying Rent

When you land on property owned by another player, the owner collects rent from you in accordance with the list printed on the Title Deed card.

Houses

When you own all of the properties in a color-group, you may buy houses from the Bank and erect them on those properties.

Hotels

When a player has four houses on each property of a complete color-group, he/she may buy a hotel from the Bank and erect it on any property of that color-group.

Bankruptcy

You are declared bankrupt if you owe more than you can pay either to another player or to the Bank. A bankrupt player must immediately retire from the game. The last player left in the game wins.

3. *Go back to exercise 1. Were your* **predictions** *correct?*

4. *Which of the following statements are true? Write* **T** *if the statement is true and* **F** *if it is false.*

ANSWER KEY

   a. _____ $1500 is divided among the players.

   b. _____ The Banker begins play.

   c. _____ If you have four houses on all of the properties in a color-group, you may buy hotels.

   d. _____ When a player lands on an owned property, he/she may buy it and put a house on it.

   e. _____ The player who is left with money after everyone goes bankrupt is the winner.

   f. _____ Whenever a player passes Jail, he gets $200.

   g. _____ Chance and Community Chest cards are placed to-gether on the appropriate space.

   h. _____ You may buy tokens from the bank.

Writing

Preparing to Write 1: Analyzing Tone

ANSWER KEY

The style or manner of the writing is the **tone.** The tone of a personal letter, for example, is informal. The tone in technical writing, such as the Monopoly directions, is formal. However, it is not as formal as a research paper or a legal contract.

1. *Answer these questions about the use of person and pronouns in the Monopoly directions on pages 151–152.*

   a. Circle any pronouns or possessive adjectives in the selection: I, we (first person); you, your (second person); he/she/it, his/him/her, they, their/them (third person).

   b. What is the most common pronoun in these directions?

   _____

2. *Answer these questions about the sentence patterns.*

   a. Underline all of the imperatives in the Monopoly directions, for example, "<u>Place</u> the board on a table."

   b. Put a <u>squiggly</u> line under all of the simple statements, that is, sentences without *if* or time clauses.

c. Put an asterisk (*) before *if* clauses and time clauses.

d. Count the number of each type of sentence structure.

Sentence Type	Number of Occurrences
Imperatives	
Simple statements	
Complex sentences with *if* or time clauses	

e. What is the most common sentence pattern in the directions?

3. *Answer these questions about sequencing and sectioning in the reading.*

a. Are there any transition words in the text, such as *first, second, third*?

b. What technique is used to show the parts of the directions?

_____

4. *Answer these questions about the verb forms in the reading.*

a. Put a box around all of the verb phrases.

b. Count these types.
- Present tense ("The equipment **consists** of . . .")
- Modals in present tense ("You **may buy** . . .")
- Passive voice ("Each player **is given** . . .")

c. What is the most common verb structure? _____

5. *Answer these questions about the format of the game instructions.*

a. How are the headings of the directions highlighted?

_____

b. Is there indenting at the beginning of each paragraph or are the paragraphs flush left?

_____

You are a member of a work group for a game company. Your current task is to design a game board to practice some aspect of English grammar or vocabulary. For example, you may want to work on verb tenses, parts of speech, or idioms.

Complete this exercise to help plan your game.

1. In your "team" decide what aspect of English you will feature in your game.

   _____

2. Make a rough sketch of the game board.

3. How will players know who will play first?

   _____

4. Where do players begin?

   _____

5. How do they advance their game pieces?

   _____

6. What are the rewards?

   _____

7. What are the penalties?

   _____

8. How is the winner determined?

   _____

9. What is the name of the game?

   _____

10. What is the name and address of your company?

    _____

Write complete instructions for a game that you design. Include the name of the game and the equipment needed. Use a logical order of headings. If you want, make illustrations to go with your game instructions.

Editing and Rewriting

Editing for Appropriate Tone

When you write technical instructions, you need to follow the usual writing conventions for setting an appropriate formal tone.

1. *Read these guidelines.*

Guidelines for Appropriate Tone	Examples
Avoid using "I" or "we." Use second or third person pronouns. Do not switch pronouns within sentences.	If **you** pass "Go,"... If **she** passes "Go," **she** ...
Use the present tense to show what usually happens in the game.	The game **consists** of ...
You may use a modal in the present tense.	A player **may buy** hotels when ...
It often is clearer to use the passive voice, focusing on the receiver of the action rather than the doer of the action.	Each player **is given** money.
Imperatives are also a common sentence pattern in directions.	**Go** to Jail. **Go** directly to Jail. **Do not pass** "Go." **Do not collect** $200.

2. *Some of these sentences do not follow the guidelines for appropriate tone in technical instructions. Find the errors in these Monopoly rules and correct them.*

Jail

a. You landed in Jail when (1) your token landed on the space marked "Go to Jail"; (2) you drew a card marked "Go to Jail"; (3) you threw doubles three times in succession.

b. When a player is sent to Jail, you cannot collect his $200 salary in that move since, regardless of where his token is on the board, you must move it directly into Jail.

c. Your turn ends when the game sends you to Jail.

d. If you are not "sent" to Jail but in the ordinary course of play you land on that space you are "Just Visiting," you incur no penalty, and move ahead in the usual manner on his next turn.

e. You get out of Jail by (1) throwing doubles on any of your next three turns; (2) using the "Get Out of Jail Free" card if you have it; (3) purchasing the "Get Out of Jail Free" card from another player and playing it, but I never sell my card; (4) paying a fine of $50 before he rolls the dice on either of his next two turns.

f. If you did not throw doubles by your third turn, you had to pay the $50 fine.

g. We then get out of Jail and immediately move forward the number of spaces shown by our throw.

Editing Checklist

Check the Content

1. *Exchange your game instructions with a classmate. After you read your classmate's game instructions, answer these questions:*

   ❑ Do the instructions follow a logical order?
   ❑ Are all of the sections of instructions included?
   ❑ Is the name of the game, the company, and its address included?

Check the Details

2. *Now, reread your game instructions. If necessary, revise them. Add or clarify information. Then continue checking your own writing. Use these questions:*

   ❑ Are the instructions in the present tense?
   ❑ Do the subjects and verbs agree?
   ❑ Are the directions lined up along the left margin?
   ❑ Are articles and nouns correct for generalizations?

3. *Revise your writing.*

Vocabulary Log

What words or phrases would you like to remember from this chapter? Write five to ten items in your notebook. Examples are on page 12.

Grammar and Punctuation Review

Look over your writing from this chapter. What changes did you need to make in grammar and punctuation? Write them in your notebook. Review them before the next writing assignment.

Class Activity   Gaming

Choose one of the following activities to do:

1 Exchange your board games from page 155 and follow the written instructions.

2 Go to a store that sells traditional or video games. Find a game that would be a good gift for a family member or a friend. Look at the packaging and try to determine what audience the game is intended for and what the game is about. Write a description of the game and tell why it would be appropriate for the person you chose.

3 Explore gaming on the Internet. Find a game that you like and write a brief description of the game, including its address.

4 Bring in a game from your culture and teach it to your classmates.

5 Dates and Mates: Changing Patterns

In this unit, you will read and write about the way dating and marriage patterns have changed in recent years. These are some of the activities you will do:

- Write a report of survey results
- Read about creative dating
- Prepare a cost analysis
- Read about changes in dating patterns
- Read letters that ask for dating advice
- Write an opinion paper on dating issues

Chapter 13

Can Money Buy Love?

What really attracts a man to a woman? A woman to a man? In this chapter you will read about a survey that asks young people what they are looking for in a mate. You will also conduct a survey and write a lab report.

Starting Point

What Do You Prefer?

Many people have assumed that women looked for wealthy husbands while men looked for beautiful wives. What do you think?

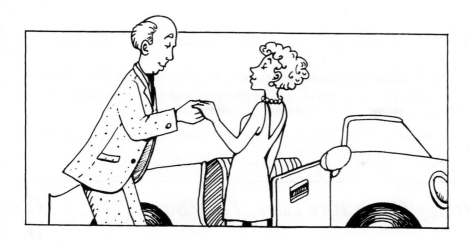

With a partner or a small group, discuss these questions:

1. Which qualities do you think women believe are the most important in choosing a husband? Rank these qualities by writing a number from 1 (highest) to 4 (lowest) in the blanks.

   _____ good looks   _____ honesty

   _____ having time for family life   _____ financial status

2. Consider these four men. Which one do you think most women would choose for a husband? Circle the letter.

   a. A very handsome man who is unfaithful to his girlfriend

   b. An average-looking man who is helpful and very eager to make people happy

   c. A rich doctor who has little time for his wife or children

   d. A high school teacher who makes $20,000 a year, loves kids, and has lots of time for family life

3. What quality do you think men look for when they consider a mate? Rank these qualities by writing a number from 1 (highest) to 3 (lowest) in the blanks.

   _____ good looks   _____ financial status

   _____ good personality

4. How about when men are choosing a date? (Rank these qualities by writing a number from 1 to 3 in the blanks.)

   _____ good looks   _____ financial status

   _____ good personality

Reading

Money Can't Buy Love

Researchers asked questions about what qualities men and women find attractive in each other. In this article, Malcolm Ritter reports on their findings.

1. *Read the following selection about research on the questions in the Starting Point.*

Money Can't Buy Love, They Say

Men who aren't rich and people who love romance stories will be happy with recent research findings. It turns out the Beatles were right: money can't buy you love. When college women chose among hypothetical men to date or marry, the attractiveness of big bucks ranked behind honesty, good looks, and having time for family life.

According to researcher Michael Cunningham of the University of Louisville in Kentucky, these results emphasize some popular, but misleading, beliefs about what attracts men and women to each other. The old theory says men look for physical attractiveness more than women do, while women seek financial resources in a mate. In the popular mind, Cunningham says, that's been simplified to "Men check out women for their figure, and women check out men for their wallet." However, the new finding emphasizes that while women may find financial resources more important than men do, money is not the main attraction.

Cunningham presented results from three experiments with college women and men. In one, 118 women chose between hypothetical men to date or marry. Each man was assigned various combinations of these elements: 1) $20,000 a year from a job or $200,000 a year from parents' winnings in a sweepstakes; 2) honesty or dishonesty; and 3) a low, medium, or high rating on dominance and competitiveness in tennis. The top choice was the man who had more money, honesty, and a medium rating in dominance and competitiveness. But money didn't do any good by itself. It only helped if the man was honest, too.

In the second study, with 52 men and 54 women, participants chose between three possible people for dates or mates. Photographs showed that the person was either physically attractive or not. Biographies showed that the person was either a millionaire or "barely scraping by," with either a good personality or a bad one. A good personality included honesty, kindness, dependability, and willingness to listen. A bad personality included shiftiness, moodiness, inflexibility, and difficulty in understanding another's problems. According to Cunningham, "It's basically nice guy vs. jerk."

When women were asked to choose a mate with one good trait and two bad ones, half picked the man with the good personality but low financial status and low physical attractiveness. Twenty-nine percent chose physical atttractiveness as the sole selling point, and 21 percent took wealth. The rankings were the same when women chose a date. Men's rankings were the same as women's for a mate, but physical attractiveness beat personality in choosing a date.

When women got a chance to pick a mate with two good traits, 81 percent went for the man with good looks plus good personality. Eleven percent went for wealth plus good personality, and 8 percent chose good looks plus wealth. The results were similar when women chose a date. Men also overwhelmingly chose beauty plus personality for a date or a mate.

The third study included 103 women. They were asked to choose among four men: a handsome rogue who cheated on his partners; an average-looking guy who was loyal, helpful, and eager to please; a rich surgeon with little time for his wife or kids; and a $20,000-a-year high school teacher who loved kids and had lots of time for family life. And the winner was…the teacher! About 60 percent chose him as a mate or a date. The wealthy, busy surgeon was picked by 15 percent.

2. Complete these **notes** about the research studies.

Researcher –
old theory: men look for
                women look for
Study 1 – (people)
women chose men with more
                and
                not important by itself.
Study 2 – (people)
women – for date or mate one trait
    %
    %
    %

men – for mate
    for date,   more
    important than
women – for date or mate two traits
    %   and
    %   and
    %   and

men –   and
    for date or mate.
Study 3 – (people)
    women chose
    over a   .

3. *Did any of the results surprise you? If so, which one?*

_____

_____

ANSWER KEY

4. *The author uses six different expressions to refer to money. Find them in the reading and place them in the correct category.*

Money	Little Money	Lots of Money

ANSWER KEY

5. *Find expressions in "Money Can't Buy Love, They Say" that are related to appearance. Are they used as adjectives or nouns? Write them here.*

<u>Adjectives</u>   **<u>Nouns</u>**

_____   _____

_____   _____

_____   _____

_____   _____

_____   _____

6. *Find the opposites of these expressions in paragraph 4 of the reading.*

ANSWER KEY

    a. difficulty in understanding another's problems

    _____

    b. shiftiness _____

    c. barely scraping by _____

7. *Writers often use other nouns, pronouns, or adjectives to* **refer** *to nouns mentioned before. What do the italicized words in each item refer to? Look in "Money Can't Buy Love, They Say."*

ANSWER KEY

    a. *That's* been simplified to, "Men check out women for their figure, and women check out men for their wallet."

    _____

    b. In *one*, 118 women chose between hypothetical men to date or marry.

    _____

    c. *It* only helped if the man was honest, too.

    _____

    d. About 60 percent chose *him* as a mate or date.

    _____

    e. *They* were asked to choose.

    _____

    f. *Half* picked the man with the good personality.

    _____

    g. Twenty-nine *percent* chose physical attractiveness as the sole selling point, and 21 percent took wealth.

    _____

8. *Complete this conversation between two friends by* **summarizing** *"Money Can't Buy Love, They Say" briefly in your own words. Give a very informal summary.*

Friend: My brother told me the other day that he's worried about whether he's going to be taken advantage of when he gets married. He's a doctor and whenever he goes out with someone who seems to like him, he's never sure whether she really likes him or whether she's just interested in his potential to make a lot of money.

You: You should tell him not to worry. I read an article recently that said that

_____

_____

_____

_____

_____

_____

Quickwriting: Important Qualities

What qualities are important to you in a date or a long-term partner? In your notebook, write for ten minutes about this question.

Targeting

Survey Questions

Carefully worded questions are important when you write a survey.

1. *Read the rules on page 167 for writing survey questions.*

Rules	Examples
Yes/no questions are the easiest kind to ask.	Are you dating someone now?
You may use adverb clauses to set a context for your question.	**If you are dating someone now,** do you want to marry that person? **When you see someone of the opposite sex,** which part of the body do you look at first? What do you look at in a person **when you first meet?**
Remember that **who** or **what** can be the subjects of questions.	**Who** has the qualities you most admire? **What** is the most important thing you look for on a first date?
You may need to "front" the preposition in a **what** question.	**At** what age do you want to get married?
Which of the following introduces choices.	**Which of the following** makes a good first impres-

2. *Write survey questions about dating that you would want to know the answers to. Complete the following question types.*

When you _____ , which

_____ ?

Which of the following _____ ?

How many _____ ?

Which kind of _____ ?

What do you _____ ?

3. *Giving choices on surveys has two advantages: choices make the questions easier to answer, and they also make it easier for you to report on the findings of your survey. What choices would you put on the survey to go with these questions? Match the choices with the question. Write the number on the line.*

Choice	**Question**
a. _____ strong, serious, funny, kind	**1.** _____ Which body size do you like best?
b. _____ yes, no	**2.** _____ What do you need to know about a person on a first date?
c. _____ thin, a little thin, average, a little heavy, heavy	**3.** _____ What do you look at in a person when you first meet?
d. _____ figure, face, height, eyes	**4.** _____ What makes a good impression on a first date?
e. _____ going to the movies, to a restaurant, dancing, outdoors	**5.** _____ What kind of personality do you like?
f. _____ younger, the same age, older, age doesn't matter	**6.** _____ Do you want to marry the person you are dating now?
g. _____ educational background, nationality, parents, work goal, financial status, age	**7.** _____ What is your favorite kind of date?
h. _____ humor, gentleness, talkativeness, honesty	**8.** _____ How old are the people whom you usually date?

The questions in Starting Point on page 161 were asked of American men and women. Would the results be the same for all cultures? Write a mixed-culture questionnaire about qualities that attract men and women to a mate or a date.

1. *Follow these steps to prepare your questionnaire.*

   a. Give your questionnaire a title.

   b. Decide on the introduction to the questionnaire. Let readers know the purpose of the questionnaire. Ask them to complete it.

   c. Decide on the background information you will need, for example, age, sex, native country.

   d. Decide on the qualities that your readers will rank. Keep these points in mind.

   - If questionnaires are long, people do not like answering them. Try to limit your survey to five or six questions.
   - If questions are too open-ended (for example, "What kind of man do you look for in a date?"), you will get too much variety in your answers. Give choices.

     For example, What body size do you like the best in a date?

heavy	a little thin
a little heavy	thin
average	

   - Think of your audience, the people you are interviewing. Decide if there are any questions that you should *not* include in your survey.

   e. Write a thank you sentence at the bottom of the questionnaire.

2. *Give your questionnaire to at least ten people.*

Preparing to Write 2: Organizing the Data

After you collect your questionnaires, tally the results. Then complete this preparation for the report on your survey.

Title of Questionnaire _____

Purpose of Questionnaire _____

_____

Procedure (a brief statement about the people in your survey and the kinds of questions you asked)

_____

_____

_____

_____

Data (a record of the results presented in an organized way)

_____

_____

_____

_____

_____

Calculations (a calculation of your results by percentages; for example, 50% chose good personality, 30% chose physical attractiveness; 50% of the women chose . . . , 60% of the Asian women chose . . .)

_____

_____

_____

_____

Results (a table of your results)

Conclusion (a summary of your results)

_____

_____

Write your report following the parts in Preparing to Write 2. Use headings such as Purpose, Procedure, Results, and Conclusions to show the parts of the report.

Writing a Technical Report

WRITING TIP

Technical reports are usually written in block style, without indenting.

Editing and Rewriting

Editing for Errors in Article Use

*Using the articles **a/an** and **the** correctly can be challenging.*

1. *In unit 4, chapter 11 (pages 146–147) you reviewed how to identify errors with singular count nouns. Here are some rules to remember when you make choices about articles.*

Rules	Examples
When a noun is specific, use **the.** A noun is specific • when it is mentioned the second time	A typical problem is lack of communication. **The** problem only gets worse if you don't try to communicate. *(second mention)*
• when additional information is given about it	She always wears jewelry, but she almost never wears **the** jewelry that I buy her! *(additional information)*
• when you and your listener or reader share an understanding of the noun	I get paid today. I'm going to use **the** money to pay my rent. *(shared understanding)* I'll meet you at **the** library. *(shared understanding)*
When a noun is not specific • use **a** for a singular count noun. • use **no article** for a non-count noun or for a plural count noun.	This is not **a** problem. *(singular count noun)* **Money** is less important than **happiness**. *(non-count noun)* **Problems** keep coming up. *(plural count noun)*

2. *Write **a/an** or **the**, where necessary, in the following paragraphs.*

Procedure

We wanted to know what was most important when choosing **(a)** _____ date or spouse. We surveyed 27 people between **(b)** _____ ages of 15 and 27 who were from **(c)** _____ various countries. There were **(d)** _____ equal number of men and women. **(e)** _____ first question was "When you see someone of **(f)** _____ opposite sex, which part of **(g)** _____ body do you look at first: face, body, or legs?" **(h)** _____ second question was "What do you look for when choosing **(i)** _____ date: good looks, humor, or good financial status?" Third, we asked, "When you look for **(j)** _____ person to marry, which quality is most important: good looks, honesty, or good financial status?" **(k)** _____ last two questions were about the desirable age of **(l)** _____ bride and groom at marriage. "How many years of age difference do you want in **(m)** _____ spouse: 1–4 years; 5–8 years; more than 8 years?" **(n)** _____ choices for age to get married were before 25; 25–30; or after 30.

Many people answered that they first look at **(o)** _____ face of **(p)** _____ person of **(q)** _____ opposite sex. Half of **(r)** _____ men regarded good looks as **(s)** _____ most important thing when they choose dates, but women chose humor. Only **(t)** _____ few people chose **(u)** _____ financial status. Most men and women chose honesty as **(v)** _____ most important quality when looking for **(w)** _____ spouse and only **(x)** _____ few people chose financial status. These results show us **(y)** _____ sincerity of young people and reaffirm **(z)** _____ research done by Cunningham, money can't buy you love.

Editing Checklist

Check the Content

1. *Exchange your survey report with a classmate. After you read your classmate's report, answer these questions:*

   ❏ Are all seven parts from Preparing to Write 2 on pages 170–171 included in the report?
   ❏ Does each part have a heading?

Check the Details

2. *Now, reread your report. If necessary, revise your survey. Add or clarify information. Then continue checking your own writing. Use these questions:*

   ❏ Are your sentences complete?
   ❏ Are verb tenses appropriate?
   ❏ Did you use articles correctly?

3. *Rewrite your survey report.*

Vocabulary Log

What words or phrases would you like to remember from this chapter? Write five to ten items in your notebook. Examples are on page 12.

Grammar and Punctuation Review

Look over your writing from this chapter. What changes did you need to make in grammar and punctuation? Write them in your notebook. Review them before the next writing assignment.

Chapter 14

Creative Dating

What are some ways to make dating more interesting? In this chapter you will read about men in the kitchen and some unusual ideas for dating. You will write a cost analysis of dating activities.

Starting Point

Male and Female Roles

The kitchen used to be a woman's domain and men usually stayed out of the kitchen. However, today more and more men are not only cooking, but also enjoying it.

Discuss the following with a classmate.

   a. What household chore would a man never do in your culture? A woman?
   b. Is it acceptable for men to cook in your culture?
   c. Did your father help with cooking when you were growing up?
   d. Would you feel comfortable dating a man who shared half of the cooking?

Reading 1

Wanted: Eligible Women Who Like Men Who Can Cook

More men are cooking these days. Are they really becoming liberated from their old roles, or do they know that this is what the modern woman wants?

1. *Read the selection on page 176.*

WANTED: Eligible Women Who Like Men Who Can Cook

> Jim Ettenson, 31, Rhinebeck, NY, owns cleaning service. Likes racquetball, running, cooking Chinese food, dining out, and going to movies.

> Raymond Pellicore, 38, Chicago, ornamental iron worker. Likes going to Bears and Hawks games, enjoys gourmet cooking and the simpler things in life.

Men who advertise in personal columns are invariably "handsome, athletic and intelligent," and sometimes own BMW's. But what's this cooking business?

In a recent survey of personal columns from Washington, D.C. to Chicago, from New York to Seattle, for every woman who touted her cooking skills there were at least twice as many men who thought their ability to cook was worth mentioning.

Ann Wood, owner of Ann Wood, the Matchmaker, a dating service in Washington, D.C., said a surprising number of men in their mid-30's know how to cook. "There's a generation gap that runs through the 40's somewhere," Ms. Wood said. "Older men may know how to cook but will leave it to others because of the way they were raised. At least half of the men under 35 cook. Rules are just not as rigid as they used to be."

Psychologists have fancier ways of describing what is happening. "It's a relatively low-cost way to portray oneself as being liberated," said Dr. Richard Eisler, professor of psychology at Virginia Polytechnic Institute and State University in Blacksburg, Va. "It says: I represent the new male, the one that supports feminist objectives, caring, emotional this and that."

"There are certain things that violate the male gender role norm, like running from a fight, not standing up for one's country. Cooking is not that kind of violation. It fits the female gender role but it's not a major violation of the male things to do."

Another psychologist, Dr. Herb Goldberg, from Los Angeles, is also the author of several books about men, including "The Inner Male," (New American Library, 1988). He talked about food and cooking as having "intimacy connotations," as a "form of seduction" and as a way for men to rid themselves of the macho image. "I think most sophisticated and aware men these days know that women respond well to men who don't have a macho image," he said, "that most women still have a fantasy of meeting Mr. Perfect, the surgeon who makes $300,000 a year in a very aggressive profession and comes home and cooks."

Mr. Goldberg said he thinks food "neutralizes men and makes them safer." "Women will not look at me or talk to me in the elevator unless I am carrying food," he said, "especially if it's something that has a smell or color. Then they start a conversation. They ask me if they can have a bite. They comment on the food. Unconsciously most women fear men, especially strange men."

If the men who advertised themselves as cooks are aware of these deeper motivations, they were not talking about them in recent telephone interviews. Their reasons are generally more practical.

"A lot of women nowadays appreciate somebody who can cook, who can share the responsibilities," said Raymond Pellicore, an ornamental ironworker who advertised in a recent issue of *Chicago* magazine. "I get off work around 3:30 or 4, and wouldn't it be nice for that other person to come home and have that dinner on the table. If two people are working all day long, it is ridiculous for me to assume that the woman would have dinner made and all cleaned up and I flop on the couch. I think those ideas are pretty much out the door."

But Mr. Pellicore, who also likes football and hockey, acknowledged that "a lot of women don't know how to take it when you invite them to your home for dinner." It is not something he would do on the first date, or even the fourth. "But," he said, "after that you can spend a lot more quality time at home in the kitchen learning about each other."

Jim Ettenson, who owns an office cleaning service in Rhinebeck, N.Y., described himself in *New York* magazine as a cook of Chinese food who is also interested in tennis, cycling, racquetball and running. He said most of his male friends are comfortable in the kitchen. "I wouldn't say they are great cooks, but most of them do their share as far as cooking, shopping and taking care of the kids," he said. "I don't know if it's choice or a strong female on the other end and you do it or they threaten you with your life."

Or as Dr. Eisler put it: "Men are aware of the fact that women want a different product. They want a man who doesn't conform to the old ways, who wants to be in control and determine how, when and where. They want men who engage in more androgynous activities."

If most of these men have found cooking skills are a plus, for some they are a barrier. Larry Kaplowitz, N.J., who advertised in New York magazine, said: "A lot of the women who responded felt intimidated by my cooking. They would say, "'Gee I don't cook,' or 'I'll do the dishes.'"

2. Use the **context** of the reading to decide if the italicized words are used correctly. Write **T** if the sentence is a correct use of the word from the reading; write **F** if it is false.

ANSWER KEY

a. _____ *Personal columns* are a way to meet people. [1]

b. _____ The differences between men and women is called *the generation gap*. [3]

c. _____ If male and female roles are *rigid,* it means men don't do women's work and women don't do men's work. [3]

d. _____ A *fancier* way of describing something is a more sophisticated way. [4]

e. _____ *Macho* men are very masculine and fit a traditional idea of what a man should be. [6]

f. _____ *Androgynous* means clearly male or female. [12]

g. _____ *Intimidated* women were comfortable being in the kitchen with men who could cook. [13]

3. Discuss with a classmate what the author means when she says the following:

a. food and cooking have intimacy connotations

b. food and cooking are a form of seduction

c. food neutralizes men

d. cooking skills are a barrier

4. Grouping key expressions in a reading will help you understand the topic. Cross out two expressions in this group that do not relate to the topic of the reading.

ANSWER KEY

gender norm	fighting	male role
being liberated	feminist	being patriotic
macho image	male cooks	

5. **Take notes** about the research studies. Complete the chart on page 178. List all of the people mentioned in the reading, their occupations, and their ideas and feelings about the topic.

ANSWER KEY

Person	Occupation	Ideas and Feelings
Ann Wood	owner of a matchmaking company	men in their 30's are less rigid about cooking than older men

6. *Look at the chart in exercise 5 and* **summarize** *the main points of the selection.*

_____

_____

_____

_____

_____

Reading 2

Climbing Trees Together

Out of money and tired of dinner or movie dates? Here are some different ideas for dating.

1. *Read the following selection.*

Climbing Trees Together

Looking at stars, having a picnic indoors, test driving new cars—do these sound like typical dates? Probably not, but they should be, according to David Coleman, Director of Student Activities at the University of Cincinnati. A few years ago, Coleman realized that many young people at his school were not dating or not enjoying dating. Many of them couldn't think of anything new to do on a date. Coleman began workshops to help students find interesting options for dating. His workshops became so popular that now he travels around the country, reaching thousands of young people at various universities. Students find his workshops positive and uplifting at a time when most young people are worried about violence and AIDS.

Coleman says people are usually not creative when planning dates. The first or second date is usually a movie followed by dinner at a restaurant. These two choices can make people uncomfortable. Why? You can't communicate at a movie, and then you have to communicate while you are eating. Coleman recommends dates that take the attention off the couple.

Here are some of the ideas from his workshops:

- Climb trees together.
- Visit significant places for one another and explain why they're significant.
- Visit a nearby college campus.
- Make homemade ice cream and invite friends to bring toppings.
- Go to the airport and watch planes land and take off.
- Take a walk in a graveyard in the daytime.
- Go to a pick-your-own orchard and pick fruit.
- Rearrange your rooms.
- Visit flea markets.
- Make tapes of favorite music.
- Cook dinner for each other.
- Go for a drive in the country.

Coleman recommends these kinds of dates because they focus on activities rather than on the couple. Another plus to the ideas above is that they usually cost less money than a typical date!

2. **Infer** the answers to these questions about the reading.

ANSWER KEY

   a. According to the reading, all of the following are true EXCEPT
1. Creative dating is usually less expensive than typical dating.
2. Students have problems thinking of new things to do on dates.
3. It's hard to talk to a new date over dinner.
4. Movie plus dinner dates are usually a comfortable way to begin dating.

b. Part of the success of Coleman's workshops is that
   1. students come away feeling good about his ideas.
   2. he emphasizes the dangers of AIDS.
   3. he has reached thousands of students across the United States.
   4. many students share a feeling of uneasiness about dating.

3. *Match these words with their definitions. Write the numbers on the lines.*

a. ____ flea market	**1.**	important
b. ____ significant	**2.**	a place where the dead are buried
c. ____ toppings	**3.**	a place where people buy and sell used items cheaply
d. ____ graveyard	**4.**	things that go on top of something
e. ____ orchard	**5.**	a large area of fruit trees

4. *Which of the ideas for creative dates in "Climbing Trees Together" sound good to you? Which would you not want to do? Why? Discuss your preferences with a partner or a small group.*

5. *Read what one woman wrote in answer to the question "What was your most memorable date?"*

Lunch among the Lupines

I was 16 and my high school sweetheart and I had planned a bike ride into the countryside in Southern California. We got up early, the weather wonderfully warm.

We started riding into the farming area—small roads with citrus orchards on both sides. I have never smelled the air so sweet or seen the orange blossoms so abundant.

Wildflowers covered the hills. The place we chose to stop and have lunch was lavender with lupine.

I proudly unpacked the food. We had ham and cheese sandwiches, a bag of Cheese Puffs, and chocolate-chip cookies I had baked because they were his favorite.

I can still see his face and feel that sun shining upon us. This was an innocent time of pure love and the temptation of being alone—finally.

This young man and I dated many years and parted. However, years later, after many elegant meals, none can compare with that one, and I bet he would agree.

6. **Apply information** from "Climbing Trees Together" to the situation in exercise 5. What was creative about this date?

_____

_____

_____

• •

Writing

Preparing to Write: Brainstorming

In unit 2, you **brainstormed** ideas. Remember that brainstorming is a way to explore a topic. These exercises will help you find out what your ideas are about creative dating.

1. *Put a check (✓) next to the items that you consider to be inexpensive, creative dates.*

_____ go to the movies

_____ look at each other's baby pictures

_____ go to a bar

_____ take your date to visit one of your friends

_____ have a picnic indoors

_____ run together in the rain

_____ go to a dance

_____ take a demonstration martial arts class together

_____ rent a video

_____ go to a museum

_____ take photographs of the season

_____ make a video together

_____ test-drive a new car at a car lot

2. *What ideas could you add to the list in exercise 1? What was your most interesting, inexpensive date or the most fun you and your friends have had together? Where did you go? What did you do?*

3. *Brainstorm some creative date possibilities in your area.*

4. *Choose three date ideas for a deeper analysis.*

5. Prepare a cost analysis sheet comparing the three date ideas from exercise 4 with more traditional dates, such as dinner, a movie, or dancing. Include such items as the activity, necessary preparation, the time of day, the length of the activity, and the cost.

6. Decide on the clearest format to display the information in your cost analysis. See chapter 4, pages 52–56, for guidelines on clear formatting of charts.

Writing a Cost Analysis

Write your cost analysis in chart form. Be sure to include an introduction to the chart.

Editing and Rewriting

EDITING TIP

Check to make sure the items in your chart are in consistent format.

Editing Checklist

Check the Content

1. Exchange your cost analysis with a classmate. After you read your classmate's cost analysis, answer these questions:

   ❏ Is there enough information about the activities?
   ❏ Is there an introduction to the chart?
   ❏ Is the chart easy to read?

Check the Details

2. Read your own cost analysis again. If necessary, revise it. Add or change details. Then continue checking your analysis. Use these questions:

   ❏ Are the words in the chart in consistent format?
   ❏ Is the punctuation and capitalization parallel?

3. Revise your writing.

Vocabulary Log

What words or phrases would you like to remember from this chapter? Write five to ten items in your notebook. Examples are on page 12.

Grammar and Punctuation Review

Look over your writing from this chapter. What changes did you need to make in grammar and punctuation? Write them in your notebook. Review them before the next writing assignment.

Chapter 15

Lifting Taboos

Many women are not only dating younger men today, but they are also marrying them. Why is this happening? In this chapter you will read about changes and problems within certain dating patterns and write a summary.

Starting Point

Mixed Relationships

1. *Look at these pictures of people on dates. Which age relationship is common in your culture? Which would you rarely see?*

2. With a partner, write some aspects of dating that are potential problems for these groups of people.

single parents _____

_____

preteens (10–12 year olds) _____

_____

coworkers _____

_____

couples many years apart in age _____

_____

cross-cultural couples _____

_____

3. Compile your list of issues on the board and discuss them with the class.

Reading 1

. . . .

Love through the Ages

December–May (older man–younger woman) relationships have been around for centuries. What explains this new twist: May–December (younger man–older woman) relationships?

1. Read the following selection.

Love through the Ages

[1] Not so many years ago, it was uncommon and unacceptable for an older woman to date a younger man. Today women in the United States are not only dating younger men, they are marrying them. In fact, 23.5 percent of all marriages are with younger men, and in the 35 to 44-year-old age group, 41 percent follow this trend. One dating agency in Los Angeles that specializes in this kind of arrangement has 6,000 clients, 70 percent of whom are men. Why is this happening?

[2] One reason is the lifting of a number of taboos in society. In the past it was taboo to date someone of another race, another religion, another country, as well as for a woman to date a younger man. The rules are not so rigid today. Since there are many single younger men out there and women usually outlive men, for many women it makes sense to date a younger man. In addition, older women say younger men are more in tune with women emotionally than men their own age.

[3] However, the most significant influence on this trend comes from women's financial independence. Many women have careers. They are active, exercising and staying more physically fit than women at 40 did even a generation ago. They are not looking for financial security from older men as they used to. This self-confidence is attractive to younger men—even more important to some men than being with a young-looking woman. Younger men say they like older women because they are confident enough to interact with the men as equals.

2. *Complete these items, according to the reading.*

   a. Put the paragraph number next to the **topic.**

   _____ why men are attracted to older women

   _____ statistics on a new trend in dating

   _____ why women are attracted to younger men

   b. Complete the **main idea** of "Love through the Ages." Circle the number of the best choice.

   More women are dating and marrying younger men because
   1. these men make more money.
   2. it's more acceptable and common for older women to date younger men.
   3. women are not dependent on men for money.
   4. taboos no longer apply.

   c. According to the reading, _____ of women are marrying younger men.
   1. 70%
   2. 23.5%
   3. 41%

    d. In paragraph 1, "this kind of arrangement" means
       1. a dating agency.
       2. clients dating.
       3. younger men marrying older women.
       4. younger men dating older women.

3. *Match these words with their definitions. Write the correct number on the blank line.*

ANSWER KEY

a. _____ uncommon

b. _____ taboo

c. _____ unacceptable

d. _____ self-confidence

e. _____ lifting

f. _____ rigid

g. _____ in tune

h. _____ trend

i. _____ physically fit

j. _____ financial security

1. believing in one's own ability

2. having enough money to live on

3. in agreement with

4. in good shape

5. not typical

6. not welcome

7. pattern

8. strongly unacceptable to society

9. taking away

10. very strict; not changing

Quickwriting: Opinion

What problems do differences in ages cause in relationships? What is your opinion of older women dating younger men? Of older men dating younger women? Write on this topic for ten minutes in your notebook.

Reading 2

....

Dr. Love

Many people write to Dr. Love for advice about dating problems.

1. *As you read the situations on the next page, consider how Dr. Love would reply.*

Letters to advice columnists do not give the real name of the writer in order to provide them with privacy. It is customary to give the name of the city and an adjective to describe the person.

Dr. Love

Dear Dr. Love:

I am a newly divorced 35-year-old coming out of a very difficult 15 years of marriage. I feel like an innocent when it comes to dating. The rules have changed a lot. I recently met a very interesting man and would love to go out with him, but I don't think he'll ever ask me out. He seems shy. Should I take the first step? Should I call him? When I was young and dating, girls never called boys. I am afraid he'll think I'm being too forward.

Old-fashioned in Detroit

Dear Dr. Love:

My parents have been divorced for less than one year, and my mom is already dating. In fact, in the past six months she has gone out with three different guys. I don't like any of them. I feel very uncomfortable when they come to our house. Sometimes she comes home so late, I get worried about her. Dad was the one who wanted the divorce. Why is she doing this?

Worried in St. Paul

Dear Dr. Love:

I am the Finance Manager of a large software company. My job is very demanding and I don't have a lot of time to get out and meet men. Recently I hired a very interesting man to join our department and I have been very pleased with his work. In fact, I have been pleased with everything about him! I enjoy all of our interactions at work and would love to see him socially. He interacts with me as if he finds me attractive, too, and I think he is waiting for some indication that I am interested in dating. However, since I am his boss, I wonder if it's a good idea to get involved with one of my employees. What do you think?

Uncertain in Savannah

Dear Dr. Love:

I met a very interesting woman about two months ago. I'll call her Marilyn. We've been seeing each other twice a week ever since. The problem is that I am a better cook than she is. When our dates are at her house, mealtime is a disaster. She gets very nervous and irritable in the kitchen but insists that I stay out of the preparations. The meals are dreadful and I can't help telling her about it. Those evenings often end up in ridiculous arguments. What should I do? I don't want to stop dating her because she is the brightest woman I've met in a long time. I love talking to her but her cooking is hard to digest!

Perplexed in Portland

2. *Match the previous letters from readers with possible pieces of advice from Dr. Love. Write the writer's location in the blank. More than one piece of advice may apply to each letter.*

a. _____Portland_____ People grow more from praise than from criticism.

b. _____ Imagine the worst case scenario: How comfortable would you feel at work if you had dated for a while and then broke up?

c. _____ It is very acceptable for single parents to date.

d. _____ Preparing food for someone is an expression of good feelings.

e. _____ Talk to your mother about your feelings about the men she dates.

f. _____ What is the worst thing that can happen if you show your interest? What do you have to lose?

g. _____ Be careful. If you have misinterpreted this man's interest and he feels pressured to go out with you because of your position, the situation could be considered sexual harassment, which is illegal.

h. _____ These days it is not unusual for women to take the first step.

i. _____ If you date this man and he gets raises or promotions, what will your other employees think of you?

3. *With a partner, discuss advice you would give for each letter written to Dr. Love.*

Reflect on Reading

In exercise 3 you **synthesized information.** When you are solving problems, you need to analyze the facts and use your background knowledge to think in original ways. This process is synthesizing, which is an important critical thinking skill.

Targeting

Ways to Express Reasons

You can express the reasons for your opinions in different ways.

1. *Read these rules for expressing reasons.*

Rules	Examples
Use these subordinate conjunctions to introduce a reason clause: *because, since, considering that, now that*	She should call him **because/since** she has nothing to lose from it. **Considering that** she has nothing to lose from it, she should call him. **Now that** her mom is dating, they need to have a talk about it.
Use these prepositions to introduce a reason phrase: *because of, due to, owing to, on account of, in view of*	**Because of** his age, his parents shouldn't worry about it. **Due to** the large number of divorces, many single parents are dating.

2. *Give advice regarding the problems in the letters to Dr. Love and include a reason clause or phrase.*

(Old-fashioned in Detroit) _____

_____

(Perplexed in Portland) _____

_____

(Worried in St. Paul) _____

_____

(Uncertain in Savannah) _____

....

A good way to develop your ideas is to hear what other people think about an issue.

In a small group, complete the chart as you discuss these issues.

Issue	*Why They Should*	*Why They Should Not*
Should children under 16 date?		
Should parents influence the people their children date?		
Should women date much younger men?		
In a relationship should men take over traditionally female roles, such as cooking and cleaning?		
Should a single parent's children be a higher priority than the person the parent is dating?		

Writing an Opinion

Write an opinion paper arguing for or against one of the dating problems that you discussed in Preparing to Write on page 191. Introduce the topic in the first paragraph. Include a thesis statement of the opinion that you support. Here are two examples of thesis statements:

Children under 16 should not date.

Parents should not influence their children's decisions about who to date.

Editing and Rewriting

More Editing for Articles

(ANSWER KEY)

Review the editing rules for articles on page 172. Then supply the missing articles for this selection.

Long-Lost Lovers

(1) _____ recent study of (2) _____ lovers reuniting after many years shows that those first romantic relationships in our lives can be the strongest. Dr. Nancy Kalish, (3) _____ psychology professor at Sacramento State University, surveyed (4) _____ couples who were in (5) _____ relationships the second time around. Of those who had renewed (6) _____ relationship with (7) _____ long-lost lover, 60% remained together. Many of these couples had been separated for (8) _____ decades, been married many years to someone else, and had changed greatly in appearance. According to Kalish, "These people are romantic and they are (9) _____ risk takers. They talk about finding their soul mates, they talk about finding the love of their lives."

Some of the subjects in the study had been childhood friends and enjoyed (10) _____ companionship of having grown up together. In other cases, a first love occurred during the happiest period of (11) _____ person's life. Later, after experiencing (12) _____ disappointments, people hoped to regain the earlier happiness.

Renowned psychologist Joyce Brothers noted that the traits
(13) ——————— people find attractive in others are formed at
(14) ——————— early age. "The characteristics we find appealing
and interesting are always there, even years later, even when fate
may break up **(15)** ——————— relationship or when they move to
(16) ——————— different part of the world."

Editing Checklist

Check the Content

1. *Exchange your opinion paper with a classmate. After you read your classmate's opinion, answer these questions:*

   - ❑ Is there a thesis statement?
   - ❑ Are there enough details and support for the thesis statement?

Check the Details

2. *Read your own opinion paper again. If necessary, revise it. Add or change details. Then continue checking your writing. Use these questions:*

   - ❑ Is the simple present used for facts and general truths?
   - ❑ Did you use reason expressions correctly?
   - ❑ Are articles used correctly?

3. *Rewrite your opinion paper.*

Vocabulary Log

What words or phrases would you like to remember from this chapter? Write five to ten items in your notebook. Examples are on page 12.

Grammar and Punctuation Review

Look over your writing from this chapter. What changes did you need to make in grammar and punctuation? Write them in your notebook. Review them before the next writing assignment.

Class Activity   Dating and Mating

Choose one of the following to do.

1 Write letters to Dr. Love with dating dilemmas. Sign the letters anonymously. Exchange them with your classmates and write responses, either serious or humorous.

2 Brainstorm an issue related to Changing Patterns. With a group of students, decide how to learn more about this topic (library research, interview, observations). Report back to your classmates about your findings on this issue. Use appropriate visuals (posters, charts, photos) to make your report more formal.

6 Beyond Your Limits

In recent years, "adventure sports" have become more popular. What accounts for this popularity? In this unit you will read about adventure sports and consider what makes some people more willing to take risks than others.

These are some of the activities you will do:

- Read about why some people like to engage in dangerous sports
- Read about acute altitude sickness and other dangers of sports
- Write short-answer responses
- Read about the benefits of sports
- Write an opinion paper about sports

Chapter 16

Risk Takers

Why do some people love to jump from airplanes and climb to dangerous heights? In this chapter you will read about what makes people take risks.

Starting Point

Adventure Sports

Adventure sports usually involve some risk. Are you a person who likes to take risks?

1. *Can you figure out why the activities in these photos are called adventure sports? Work with a classmate. Identify each sport and explain the risk that is involved. Would you like to try these activities?*

2. *Do you like to take risks? Respond to these statements to find out. If you agree with the statement, circle **T** (True). If you disagree, circle **F** (False).*

1. I usually begin a new job without much planning about how I will do it. **T F**
2. I usually think about what I am going to do before I do it. **T F**
3. I often do things on impulse. **T F**
4. I very seldom spend much time on the details of planning. **T F**
5. I like to have new and exciting experiences and sensations, even if they are a little frightening. **T F**
6. Before I begin a complicated job, I make careful plans. **T F**
7. I would like to take off on a trip with no planned routes or timetable. **T F**
8. I tend to change interests frequently. **T F**
9. I'll try anything once. **T F**
10. I would like to be on the move and travel a lot, with lots of change and excitement. **T F**
11. I sometimes do "crazy" things just for fun. **T F**
12. I like to explore a strange city or section of town by myself, even if it means getting lost. **T F**
13. I prefer friends who are excitingly unpredictable. **T F**
14. I often get so carried away by new and exciting things and ideas that I don't think of possible complications. **T F**
15. I like "wild," uninhibited parties. **T F**

Scoring: Score one for each item answered "true" except for No. 2 and No. 6. Score one for "false" answers to Nos. 2 and 6. Find your level of risk taking:

Men		Women
0–5	very low	0–4
6–7	low	5–6
8–10	average	7–9
11–13	high	10–12
14–15	very high	13–15

Reading

Risk Takers

What makes people want to jump out of airplanes and climb mountains? Is it body chemistry or just personality?

1. *Read the following selection on page 198.*

Risk Takers

READING TIP

If you see an unfamiliar word, look to see if the writer gives a definition.

[1] Have you ever gone skydiving, gone mountain climbing, or raced a fast car? Why are some people willing to risk death for a high feeling when others find everyday life risky enough? Typically, these thrill-seekers are more easily bored but more focused than the rest of us. They might even be a little smarter than the rest of us, although they don't necessarily live longer! At other times in history, these people would have been explorers or immigrants.

[2] *Adrenaline* is a chemical the body makes when people feel fear. People who jump, kayak, sail, fly, ski, or otherwise risk themselves get an adrenaline rush. This adrenaline rush makes them feel more intensely alive. Some researchers believe this chemical rush can become addictive.

[3] Is it this addiction that makes people take risks? Or are some people just born to seek thrills? Some researchers believe risk taking is linked to a gene, a basic element that controls cell development. This gene allows the brain to respond to a chemical messenger called *dopamine*. Earlier experiments showed that without enough dopamine, animals lost their aggressiveness. They also lost their interest in sex and their desire for exploration. The latest research suggests that humans who have the dopamine-receptor gene, about 15 percent of the population, are significantly more extravagant, excitable, and impulsive. However, researchers caution that genes don't determine our lives. Genes may control about 60 percent of our risk taking. The rest is up to us.

[4] Not all risks are attractive to risk takers. Oddly enough, some people who are not afraid to hang glide or mountain climb are more cautious about asking their bosses for a raise or starting a new business. There are also risk differences between men and women. Women are more likely than men to perceive not wearing a seat belt as risky. Men are more likely to find marriage risky. Researchers believe the differences are due to the sex hormones. The male hormone *testosterone* seems to be the cause of much risky behavior in men, especially in young men.

[5] Other researchers believe women aren't afraid to take risks. They just take fewer risks because they feel a strong responsibility to others—family and community. Women are taught as children to be

more cautious and take fewer risks. They also know they are smaller and less strong than men. However, when women and men have the same education level, their risk-taking differences are much smaller.

2. *Look at these expressions from the reading. What topic were they connected to in "Risk Takers"? Write them in the chart below.*

ANSWER KEY

asking for a raise   racing fast cars   getting married

more focused people   15% of the population   body chemical

adrenaline   not wearing a seat belt   more easily bored

✓ mountain climbing   skydiving   extravagant

usually male   chemical messenger   excitable

desire for exploration   dopamine   intensely alive

willing to risk death

Risky Behavior	Chemical Reactions	Thrill-Seekers
mountain climbing		

3. **Taking notes in a diagram** *is a helpful academic reading skill. Complete these diagrams with information from paragraphs 2 and 3 in the reading.*

ANSWER KEY

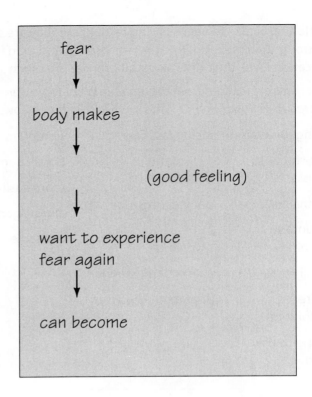

fear

↓

body makes

↓

(good feeling)

↓

want to experience
fear again

↓

can become

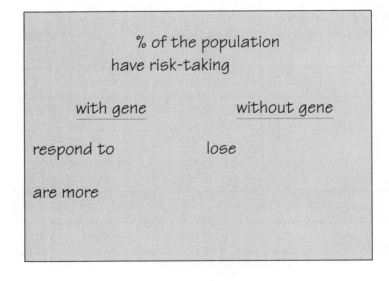

% of the population
have risk-taking

with gene   without gene

respond to   lose

are more

4. *Read carefully and **analyze.** Read "between the lines" to answer these* why *questions:*

4. *Read carefully and **analyze.** Read "between the lines" to answer these* why *questions:*

ANSWER KEY

a. Why do you think thrill-seekers are more easily bored but more focused than people who are not risk takers?

_____

_____

_____

b. Why are immigrants considered risk takers?

_____

_____

_____

c. Why do researchers believe there is a relationship between risk and dopamine?

_____

_____

_____

d. Why do researchers think testosterone plays a part in risk taking?

_____

_____

_____

e. Why do some researchers believe women aren't afraid to take risks?

_____

_____

_____

5. *What can you* **infer** *from "Risk Takers"? Write* **T** *next to the true statements and* **F** *next to the false statements.*

a. _____ A person who kayaks has a lower chance of death than a person who doesn't.

b. _____ If people are given the chemical dopamine, they will be willing to take more risks.

c. _____ Many people who skydive are not afraid to take risks at work or in their relationships.

d. _____ Women are less afraid of taking marriage risks than men.

e. _____ Older men have more testosterone than younger men.

f. _____ Aggressiveness is necessary to be a risk taker.

g. _____ Skiing is a risky sport.

h. _____ Men don't feel as responsible for family and community as women do.

Reflect on Reading

In exercise 4 you **analyzed** the text. Analyzing is a critical thinking skill. When you analyze a text, you break it into parts and identify its organization, draw conclusions, or make generalizations. You answer the question *Why?* What kind of reading do you do that requires you to analyze and answer the question *Why?* Discuss this with a partner.

Targeting

Collocations

Collocations are words that commonly go together.

1. *Scan "Risk Takers" for the word* risk *in any of its forms. Underline those words and any phrases that occur with them.*

2. *Complete this chart with your "risk" phrases.*

As a verb	As an adjective (including nouns acting as adjectives)
As a noun	
risk taking	

Are you comfortable taking risks? What about physical risks? Have you ever tried a dangerous sport or activity? Write in your notebook for ten minutes about yourself as a risk taker.

Quickwriting: Your Experience

Vocabulary Log

What words or phrases would you like to remember from this chapter? Write five to ten items in your notebook. Examples are on page 12.

Chapter 17

First Aid on the Mountain

Mountain climbing can be dangerous. In this chapter you will read about one of the most common dangers of mountain climbing and write answers to short-answer questions.

Starting Point

Emergency Care

What would you do if you were on a mountain, miles away from any help, and one of your companions became ill?

1. *If you were climbing a mountain and a fellow climber showed these symptoms, what would you do? Discuss the following symptoms and your ideas in a small group. Complete the chart.*

Symptom	First Aid
vomiting	
a headache	
trouble with breathing	
extreme tiredness	
slight dizziness	

2. *Which drink would be best to give someone who did not feel well on the mountain? Circle one.*

a soft drink	coffee
beer or other alcohol	fruit juice
water	milk

3. *Match the body organ or system with the adjective that describes it.*

a. _____ pulmonary   **1.** lungs

b. _____ cerebral   **2.** heart, arteries, veins

c. _____ respiratory   **3.** heart and lungs

d. _____ circulatory   **4.** brain

Reading

Altitude Sickness

One of the serious dangers of mountain climbing is a sickness caused by the change in altitude.

1. *Preview the reading. Think about these questions as you skim.*

What is the title of the reading?

Are there any highlighted words (for example, bold or italics)?

What are the headings?

What do you expect to learn from this reading?

2. *Now read the selection on pages 206–207, but don't worry about unfamiliar vocabulary.*

READING TIP

Previewing a reading by *skimming* helps you understand a difficult reading. When you skim, look at the text quickly and find the general idea. Look at headings and the first sentences of paragraphs. Don't worry about reading individual words or understanding details at this point.

Air Pressure

At a constant altitude, the amount of oxygen in the air remains the same. It does not vary much with the temperature, time of day, season, or any other typical environmental change. Your major body systems become accustomed to this. For example, your rate of respiration and the number of red blood cells in your circulation are in balance with your environment.

An increase in altitude by foot, car, plane, or hot-air balloon changes the atmospheric environment around you. The higher you go, the less oxygen there is. At about 18,000 feet above sea level, air pressure is reduced by 50%.

Physical Effects of Changes in Air Pressure

As you change altitude gradually, your body compensates with gradual changes. You can move from sea level to about 8000 feet with little effect. In the short term, there will be an increase in how quickly you breathe. There will also be chemical changes (elevated pH) in the blood. If you stay several days, your kidneys will rebalance the pH of the blood. This will resettle your system to your new environment.

Each time you go higher, your body compensates and rebalances again. Over the course of weeks, there are more physiological changes, like producing more red blood cells. However, there is a limit to how much your body can compensate.

Individual Differences in Adapting to Altitude Changes

The ability to adapt to a higher altitude is different from person to person. It appears to have no relationship to physical fitness or gender. However, a climber's ability will decrease if alcohol or depressant drugs are in his or her system. Dehydration or over-exertion also affects a climber's ability and speed in adapting to the change in altitude.

Guidelines for Healthy Climbing

The best way to adapt to higher altitude is to take your time, drink a lot of liquids, stay away from alcohol and depressants, and take it easy. Allow your normal compensatory mechanisms the time necessary to work by climbing in stages. Climb no faster than your body can adapt. Do not overexert on the first day at the new altitude. Plan to remain for two or three days before going higher. If you pay attention to what your body is trying to tell you, you should be able to avoid the more severe forms of altitude sickness.

Acute Altitude Sickness

When you don't have enough oxygen, severe or acute altitude sickness develops. Blood leaks from tiny blood vessels and tissues swell throughout the body. The organs most seriously affected by this are the brain and lungs. These are symptoms of the medical problem we call Acute Mountain Sickness (AMS). The two major components are called High Altitude Pulmonary Edema (HAPE), and High Altitude Cerebral Edema (HACE).

Assessment of AMS

In the early stages, symptoms are the result of the chemical effects of having less oxygen per breath and the work your body has to do to compensate for this. Later, more serious symptoms appear as swelling, or

edema, develops throughout the body. Its effects are first noticed in the lungs and brain. Severe altitude sickness includes the effects of fluid in the lungs and increased pressure in the brain.

A mild headache easily relieved by aspirin or ibuprofen is typical of *Mild AMS*. There will also be slight nausea with little or no vomiting. The patient may experience slight dizziness, loss of appetite, and mild tiredness. There is usually some degree of insomnia and increased shortness of breath on exertion.

Moderate AMS produces severe headaches that aspirin or ibuprofen cannot relieve. There is also frequent vomiting and moderate tiredness.

Severe AMS is a life-threatening emergency. The patient will show changes in consciousness. He or she may become ataxic (unable to walk straight), and severely tired and short of breath, even at rest. There may be a cough and the patient may appear cyanotic (blue or pale) and much weaker than others in the group.

The symptoms of Severe AMS can be confused or mixed with those of other problems such as hypoglycemia (low blood sugar), dehydration, hypothermia, hyperthermia, and exercise exhaustion. All of these problems can cause a decrease in muscular performance and efficiency and changes in levels of consciousness. Under most field conditions, the most practical approach is to include all five problems as possible causes.

Treatment of AMS

With the treatment of AMS, two days of prevention are worth 4000 feet of cure. The key is to recognize the mild forms and allow your body time to adapt.

Mild AMS is treated with mild pain relievers such as aspirin, ibuprofen, or Tylenol. The patient should avoid sedatives like alcohol or narcotic drugs, which can affect respiration. This is the time to rest at the present altitude, or descend to a lower altitude until the body adapts.

Moderate AMS is treated with pain medication, rest, and avoidance of sedatives. In addition, if possible, immediately descend 1000-2000 feet. The patient should be closely observed for increasing severity of symptoms. Be prepared for an emergency descent if symptoms get worse. Supplemental oxygen and steroids (by physician's prescription) may be helpful, if available.

All of the techniques covered for mild and moderate forms can be used for *Severe AMS*, including an immediate descent. Try not to exert the patient, but there should be no delay in descent.

3. Look at these groups of words. Circle the term that is the **category** in each group.

a. brain   heart   lungs   (body organs)   kidneys

b. headache nausea vomiting symptoms dizziness
insomnia coughing shortness of breath loss of appetite

c. medical conditions edema acute altitude sickness hypo-glycemia

d. time of day temperature season of year environmental changes

e. climbing slowly maintaining hydration ways to adapt to higher altitudes avoiding depressants and alcohol taking it easy

f. producing more red blood cells rebalancing pH in blood increasing respiration compensatory mechanisms

4. Arrange these adjectives in order of degree.

severe   acute   moderate   slight   mild   frequent

slight

5. Go back and **scan** "Acute Mountain Sickness" to find the answers to these questions.

a. At what altitude is air pressure reduced by 50 percent?

_____

b. How far can you climb from sea level without feeling the many effects of changes in air pressure? _____

c. Which two body organs are first affected by altitude sickness?

_____ and _____

d. What does AMS mean? _____

e. What are the three levels of AMS called? _____ ,

_____ , and _____

f. What are two symptoms of Mild AMS? _____

g. What are two symptoms of Moderate AMS? _____

h. What are two symptoms of Severe AMS? _____

6. *Taking notes in a chart* *will help you understand the information in* *"Acute Mountain Sickness" better. Complete this chart with treat-* *ment for the three levels of AMS.*

Level of AMS	*Treatment*

7. *In "Acute Mountain Sickness,"* **scan** *the paragraph indicated in brack-* *ets to complete this chart of* **context clues, definitions,** *and* **terms.**

Term	Context Clue	Definition
elevated pH [3]	(parentheses)	chemical change in the blood
slight [9]	with	
acute [7]		severe
ataxic [11]		
 [11]		blue or pale
hypoglycemia [12]		
 [14]	like	alcohol or narcotic drugs
aspirin, ibuprofen, or Tylenol [14]		

Targeting

Prefixes and Roots

Learning common prefixes and roots in English helps you decode the meanings of unfamiliar words more quickly.

1. *Look at the definitions of these words beginning with the same prefix. What do you think each of the prefixes means?*

a. *rebalance*   to make stable again

     resetting   to put back into original position

     remain   to stay back

     reduce   to put back in a smaller number or degree

     re- means _____ OR _____

b. *dehydrate*   to take water away from

     depressant   something that pushes down

     descend   to come down

     decrease   to take part of the size away

     de- means _____ OR _____

c. *overexertion*   to put out too much energy

     overcompensate   to give or pay too much for something

     overweight   to be too heavy

     overconfident   feeling better about yourself than you should

     over- means _____

d. *insomnia*   not being able to sleep

     inability   not being able to do something

     unadapted   not changed

     unavailable   not present or able to use

     in- and *un-* mean _____

e. *hyperthermia*   above normal body temperature

     hypothermia   below normal body temperature

     hypoglycemia   below normal blood sugar

     hyper- means _____

     hypo- means _____

2. *Look at the definitions of these words with the same root. What do you think each word root means?*

a. *physical*   related to nature

    physiology   the study of biology that deals with living organisms

    physical fitness   keeping your body in good health

    physi- means _____

b. *hydration*   an adding of water

    dehydrate   to lose water

    hydroelectric   related to the production of electricity by water power

    hydr- means _____

c. *depressant*   something that pushes down

    air pressure   the pushing down by the atmosphere

    antidepressants   drugs that work against a low mental state

    intracranial pressure   force inside the brain

    press- means _____

Writing

Preparing to Write 1: Understanding Essay Exam Questions

When you take essay exams, you need to write carefully organized answers that show you understand the course material. You also have a limited amount of time to write. Your first step in preparing to write is to analyze the question.

1. *If you found these phrases in short-answer test questions, what kind of a paragraph would you write? Label the phrases with appropriate paragraph organizational patterns.*

D: definition   CC: comparison/ contrast   C-R: cause-result/ effect

CL: classification   P: process   EX: examples to prove a generalization

a. _P_ Explain the process . . .

b. ____ Define . . .

c. ____ What is the effect of . . .

d. ____ Compare . . . to . . .

e. ____ What types of . . .

f. ____ What is meant by . . .

g. ____ What are the major differences between . . .

h. ____ What are the causes of . . .

i. ____ Illustrate . . .

j. ____ Discuss the reasons for . . .

k. ____ What are the distinguishing characteristics of . . .

l. ____ What were the major factors . . .

m. ____ How is . . . divided . . .

n. ____ Explain the differences between . . .

o. ____ What does . . . mean . . .

p. ____ What factors contributed to . . .

q. ____ Why . . .

r. ____ Trace the development of . . .

s. ____ Discuss the advantages of . . . over . . .

t. ____ What has been the result of . . .

u. ____ Give examples to show that . . .

v. ____ Contrast . . . with . . .

w. ____ How does . . . work

x. ____ Classify . . .

y. ____ What differences distinguish . . . from . . .

z. ____ Name . . .

aa. ____ Explain the reasons for . . .

bb. ____ How does . . . define . . .

Preparing to Write 2: Organizing Essay Exam Responses

The second step in essay tests is to organize your response.

- Quickly write down brief notes about the information you will use in your response.
- As you look at your notes, decide what your main point is.
- Begin your answer with a topic sentence that shows that you understand the question. Include a rephrasing of the question in your first sentence.

After you have your topic sentence, your task is to support your main point.

ANSWER KEY

1. *Rephrase each question as the topic sentence of your response.*

   a. What process does your body go through if you make a gradual altitude change?

   There are five typical changes to your body due to a

   gradual altitude change. The first one is . . .

   b. What differences distinguish Mild AMS from Severe AMS?

   _____

   _____

   c. What are the three types of Acute Mountain Sickness?

   _____

   _____

   d. What does Acute Mountain Sickness mean?

   _____

   _____

   e. Discuss the steps climbers can take to avoid getting AMS.

   _____

   _____

Writing Essay Exam Responses

Write short answers to the questions in Preparing to Write 2. Use transition words or expressions to connect your ideas. The length of your response will depend on how long your instructor gives you to write. For example, if you have five questions to answer in fifty minutes, your instructor probably expects one paragraph per answer. If you have an hour to answer only one question, you should write at least a five paragraph essay.

The passive voice is often used in academic writing and official documents. Students are often uneasy about using the passive, and they tend to avoid it. Remember these rules when you use the passive voice.

1. *Read these rules for using the active voice and the passive voice.*

Rules	*Examples*
In an **active** sentence, the doer of the action is the most important part of the sentence. For this reason, it is usually the first element.	*Doer Action Receiver or Object of the action* The experienced climbers **helped** the others down the mountain. Someone **may treat** mild AMS with ibuprofen.
In a **passive** sentence, the receiver of the action is the most important part. Therefore, it is moved to the front of the sentence. The doer is moved to the receiver position, and the verb takes the form of **BE + past participle.**	*Receiver BE + p.p. by Doer or Object* The others **were helped** down the mountain by the experienced climbers. Mild AMS **may be treated** (by someone) with ibuprofen.
We also use the passive if we don't know who the doer of the action is or if we want to hide the doer.	The injured climbers **were rescued** after two days on the mountain.

2. *In the paragraphs that follow, look at the underlined verb phrases. Decide whether they should be active or passive. Correct any mistakes in the verb phrases.*

must always be considered
(a) Dehydration <u>must always be consider</u> when you <u>are exercising</u>.

(b) Many people <u>are pushed</u> themselves too far without taking in enough liquids. **(c)** Large amounts of water <u>lost</u> when you <u>are being exercised</u> in hot weather or <u>overexerting</u> yourself. **(d)** Unfortunately, you <u>may not know</u> that you <u>are</u> at the danger point until it <u>is</u> too late. **(e)** If you <u>have not been taking in</u> enough water, you <u>will become</u> very tired and <u>may even become</u> headachy, dizzy, or nauseated. **(f)** If you <u>are</u> a person who <u>sweats</u> a good deal, you <u>are</u> at risk of becoming dehydrated. **(g)** Also, if you <u>are</u> an older person, your ability to sweat <u>may have been declined</u>. **(h)** It <u>is</u> especially dangerous to exercise in clothing that <u>does not breathe</u>, such as plasticized clothes.

    (i) A large number of fluids <u>must be drunk</u> before and during physical activities. **(j)** For example, 16 ounces of water <u>should taken in</u> two hours before an activity. Six to twelve ounces <u>should drink</u> every 15 to 20 minutes during the activity. **(k)** <u>Avoid</u> caffeine and alcohol. **(l)** Your body's ability to absorb water <u>enhance</u> if the liquid <u>has</u> small amounts of sugar in it. **(m)** This <u>is</u> because muscle fatigue is delaying by maintaining a normal level of glucose in the blood.

(n) However, if you take in too much sugar, you may be experienced

bloating and cramps.

   (o) If you want a sports drink with more flavor than water, an inex-

pensive drink can make in your own home. **(p)** In a quart jar or

pitcher, dissolve 1/4 cup sugar in 1/2 cup hot water. **(q)** After the

sugar is dissolve, 1/4 cup orange juice, 1/4 teaspoon salt, and 3 1/4

cups of cold water should been added. **(r)** Stir.

Editing Checklist

Check the Content

1. *Exchange your essay exam responses with a classmate. After you read your classmate's work, answer these questions:*

   ❑ Is there a topic sentence that rephrases the question?
   ❑ Is there enough support for the topic sentence?
   ❑ Are there transition words or expressions to tie the paragraph together?

Check the Details

2. *Read your own writing again. If necessary, revise. Add or change details. Then continue checking your work. Use these questions:*

   ❑ Are your verb tenses correct?
   ❑ Are there any sentences that require the passive?

3. *Revise your writing.*

Vocabulary Log

What words or phrases would you like to remember from this chapter? Write five to ten items in your notebook. Examples are on page 12.

Grammar and Punctuation Review

Look over your writing from this chapter. What changes did you need to make in grammar and punctuation? Write them in your notebook. Review them before the next writing assignment.

Chapter 18

Playing Hard

In this chapter you will read about how sports affect our lives. You'll also write your opinion about the benefits or harm of sports.

Starting Point

Rock climbing, an adventure sport that challenges your mind and your body, has become very popular in recent years. It is growing by 50 percent a year, and one-quarter of all climbers are women.

Rock Climbing

1. *Look at the illustration of rock climbing and read the descriptions of rock-climbing experiences. Match the person with the description.*

ANSWER KEY

a. _____

I didn't really want to go to the climbing class, but my parents made me. I thought climbing was stupid, you know, something for those outdoor types. The first few days I hated it. It was really hard. But when we went up a really steep cliff, working together as a team, it was cool. I learned a lot about myself on that course. I was responsible for my teammates and we did a great job together. I'm even thinking maybe I'd like to teach other kids to climb.

b. _____

Our company recommended that all managers take the climbing course, so it started out as just another part of my job. But the experience was better than any leadership workshop I've ever attended. You have to think about each move you take. Then you know right away if you made the right decision. I learned more about teamwork and gained some good insights into myself. I'll remember these lessons the rest of my life.

c. _____

Me, a 100-pound weakling, climb a rock mountain? It was terrifying. I'm a person who never wanted to even go camping! This was really in the raw outdoors, facing all kinds of weather. I had to push and push myself to keep up with the group. I never knew I had it in me. I went beyond my limits. When I got to the top, I realized my potential. Now I feel a lot more respect for myself. I feel confident that I can do anything I set my mind to.

2. *What was each person's attitude about climbing before he or she experienced it? Underline words or expressions in their self-descriptions that show how these people felt about the experience of climbing before they went.*

3. *Underline words and expressions in the reading that show what the three climbers learned besides rock-climbing skills.*

4. *The rock climbers describe only the positive aspects of their experience. What do you think are some of the dangers of rock climbing? Talk about them with a partner.*

5. *Have you ever experienced a sports injury? If so, talk about it with a partner.*

Reading 1

....

Hazardous Sports

Each year people who participate in recreational sports are injured or even killed. Which sport do you think is the most dangerous: hang gliding, swimming, or in-line skating?

1. *Read the following one-year statistics about some typical sports.*

Hazardous Sports

Swimming

Participants: More than 63 million
Deaths: 3,400. Most were drownings. Also included in this tally are people who fell into pools, oceans, or lakes.
Injuries: About 120,000 plus an estimated 500,000 unreported jellyfish stings.

Scuba Diving

Participants: More than 2 million
Deaths: 92. Most were due to drowning, only infrequently from being trapped in a cave or wreck.
Injuries: 508 reported and verified by Dive Alert Network. Most involved "the bends."

Hang Gliding

Participants: About 50,000 flew at least once
Deaths: 9
Injuries: 315 reported to the US Hang Gliding Association, including broken ankles, feet, and arms.

Boating

Participants: More than 75 million
Deaths: 800. Most from drowning. At least half of the deaths involved alcohol consumption.
Injuries: The Coast Guard reported 3,560 in a total of 6,335.

Rock Climbing and Mountaineering

Participants: More than 200,000
Deaths: 21. Most from falling. Some climbers were swept away in avalanches.
Injuries: The American Alpine Club reported 121, including bone fractures, lacerations, frostbite, and hypothermia.

In-Line Skating

Participants: More than 19.5 million
Deaths: 28 overall, since the International In-Line Skating Association started keeping statistics in 1990. Most involved cars; none when the skater was wearing a helmet.
Injuries: An estimated 73,000 per year, including wrist sprains, lacerations, and the awful scrapes known as red rash.

Golf

Participants: 24.5 million golfers played nearly 500 million rounds
Deaths: 1. A golfer died after being struck by lightning.
Injuries: 8 golfers were struck by lightning but survived. About 38,000 suffered fire ant bites, heat stroke, muscleache and bruises—the last from being hit by golf balls.

Billiards and Pool

Participants: More than 40 million people played at least once

Deaths: None. Ever.

Injuries: The Consumer Product Safety Commission estimates 5,194 people injured themselves shooting pool. The injuries could include back strain from bending over. Or, says Theresa Daly of the American Poolplayers Association, "I guess, maybe, if you were to hit the ball off the table—you know, it is heavy—it could hit your toe, and that could cause an injury."

Bowling

Participants: 79 million people tried this air-conditioned sport

Deaths: None. "You'll get a couple of heart attacks each year, but those are people who just happen to be bowling at the time" says Mark Miller of the American Bowling Congress.

Injuries: A calculated estimate of 23,814. Mostly tendinitis, in wrist and elbow.

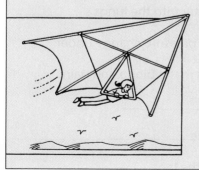  

2. *Are the statements below true or false? Write **T** for true and **F** for false. You may have to **infer** the meaning in some cases.*

a. _____ Swimming is more dangerous than hang gliding.

b. _____ Bowling can put a lot of strain on your heart.

c. _____ Extreme temperature can cause injuries when you are rock climbing.

d. _____ Most skating injuries happened when skaters were wearing helmets.

e. _____ Some scuba divers have died when ships wrecked.

f. _____ Fifty percent of all boating deaths were caused by people who were drinking alcohol.

g. _____ It is okay to golf when there is a thunderstorm as long as you are properly dressed for the weather.

h. _____ Most scuba-diving injuries are the result of being unable to escape from caves or wrecks.

i. _____ Bowling is hard on the wrists and elbows.

j. _____ The causes of billiard and pool injuries are not certain.

3. *Match these words with their definitions. If you need help, **scan** the reading to find the word in the context of the sport.*

ankle	fracture	participants	tendinitis
avalanche	frostbite	scrape	the bends
bruises	lacerations	sprain	verify
drowning			

a. people who take part in a sport _____

b. death from taking too much water into the lungs _____

c. a condition due to atmospheric pressure change under

water, characterized by bubbles in the blood and pain

in the lungs _____

d. make sure that something is true _____

e. the joint between the foot and the leg _____

f. the medical term for a break in something hard, like a

bone _____

g. damage to parts of the body exposed to extreme cold

_____

h. the medical term for cuts on the body _____

i. large amounts of snow or ice that come suddenly down a

mountain _____

j. an injury due to rubbing against something rough _____

k. the medical term for damage to a joint in the body, usually

caused by twisting _____

l. a swelling of the cord that connects muscle to bone

_____

m. discolored places where the skin has been hit by something

_____

Reading 2

Playing Hard

....

Women have become much more involved in sports in the past few decades and have benefited in several ways.

1. *Read the following selection.*

Playing Hard

[1] If girls want to grow up to be successful, they must not only work hard, but also play hard. Twenty-five years ago, the United States passed a law to require equal opportunities for women in sports. Since then, the number of female athletes has risen from 300,000 to more than two million. More girls are participating in a wider variety of physical activities than ever before in American history. The news

is full of success stories, often about how much money female athletes are finally able to make. However, the real news is the long-term benefits for girls when they begin to participate in team sports at an early age.

[2] For several years statistics have shown the positive effects for women. According to a survey by the Women's Sports Foundation (1989), female athletes score higher on standardized tests than nonathletes. They also have higher grades and are more likely to graduate from high school. Black female college athletes in one division are graduating at a rate of 58 percent compared with 41 percent for black females in the general student population (N.C.A.A. News, June 1995). The Ms. Foundation found that female athletes are less likely to suffer from depression (1991). They also significantly reduce their risk of developing breast cancer (National Cancer Institute, 1994).

[3] To add to these studies, government research in 1997 showed that being on a team had a positive effect on a girl's overall growth and development academically, physically, and emotionally. The President's Council on Physical Fitness and Sports found that female high school athletes got better grades, were less likely to drop out of school, and were more likely to go on to college than nonathletic girls. These girls experienced less stress and, as earlier studies had pointed out, they were less likely to be depressed than their nonathletic counterparts. Athletic teens had fewer health problems, such as heart disease and high levels of cholesterol. In terms of emotional development, these young women had better social skills. They also were more self-confident, had healthy self-images, and were less likely to have an unwanted pregnancy.

[4] The downside of the government's findings was the evidence that poor girls are missing out on the opportunities that physical activity and sports can provide. In addition, in spite of Title IX, there is still discrimination against girls as athletes. Fewer athletic scholarships are available for them. They tend to get the poorer facilities on campuses. Even low media coverage of women in sports hurts all girls since it keeps them from seeing strong, successful, athletic women as role models.

[5] These studies show the importance of girls' participation in team sports at an early age. Team sports will not only help them get

through the difficult teenage years, but will also help them succeed throughout life. Considering how healthy it is for girls to be athletic, a good use of public health money is to encourage girls to play hard.

2. *Cross out the words or phrases that do not fit the* **topic** *of each group. Be prepared to explain your choices.*

   a. high academic grades   ~~depression~~   good self-image

   b. research   athletes   studies   statistics

   c. fewer chronic health problems   higher incidence of breast cancer   greater chance of an unwanted pregnancy

   d. heart disease   cholesterol   breast cancer   depression

   e. benefits   positive effects   suffering

3. ***Taking notes in a chart*** *will help you understand the information in* "*Playing Hard.*" *List the studies and the results in this chart or on a separate piece of paper.*

Study (year)	Results
Women's Sports Foundation (1989)	female athletes — higher scores on standardized tests, higher grades, more likely to graduate from high school

> ### READING TIP
>
> When you take notes, use key words and noun phrases instead of complete sentences.

....

Are all sports beneficial? Do some sports have a greater effect on our lives than others? Are some sports too dangerous for young people to participate in? Is it more valuable to participate in a team sport or an individual sport?

Writing

Preparing to Write 1: Discussing Possibilities

1. *Complete this chart as you discuss these questions with your classmates.*

	Team Sports	Individual Sports	Risky Sports
What can you learn from . . . ?			
What are the negative effects of . . . ?			
In each of these categories, which sports are the most beneficial? The most harmful?			

2. *What are some of the reasons for your opinions about sports? List them with examples from your experiences.*

Reasons	Examples

Introductions

Once you know what your opinion is on a subject, how do you begin to write about it? Start with an introduction. The purpose of an introductory paragraph is to get the readers' attention so that they will want to read on. The introduction starts with an *interest catcher*. After the interest catcher, you can give a little background information to help the readers understand the topic, but this is not always necessary. Finally, state your main point, or your thesis.

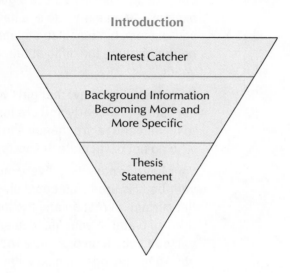

Introduction

Interest Catcher

Background Information Becoming More and More Specific

Thesis Statement

1. *Match these common, interest-catcher techniques for getting readers' attention with their examples on the following page. Complete the first column with items from the list. Underline the main idea in each example.*

surprising fact   question   description of a scene

representative case   relevant quotation

Interest-Catcher Technique	Example
a. *representative case*	According to Benita Fitzgerald Mosley, Olympic gold medalist and director of the U.S. Olympic Training Center, if you participate in sports, you gain a base of strength that stays with you throughout your life. Mosley's life is a good example. At an early age she had low self-esteem, but being an athlete helped her get through the difficult teenage years.
b.	Recent studies show that girls who begin sports at an early age are less likely to have teenage pregnancies than girls who do not participate in sports.
c.	Your heart is pounding. Every muscle in your body is tired. You could die for a flat surface to rest on and the longest drink of water in your life. You are sure you can't climb up one more rock, but you keep moving—almost without willing your body to. When you reach the top of the mountain, it's all worth it. The view is incredible. But most of all, you know you have what it takes to get to the top.
d.	Is the danger of some sports addictive? Climbing is, according to Jim Wickwire, world-class mountain climber. For him, a life with risks is worth living. One without risks is just too boring.
e.	According to an old proverb, all work and no play makes Jack a dull boy. If you really want to succeed in life, you have to play as hard as you work.

Conclusions

Students often get stuck at the end of a composition. Writing conclusions can be as difficult as writing introductions. The purpose of the concluding paragraph is to give your paper a sense of completeness. Here are some techniques for writing conclusions.

- Restate your thesis. Use different words than you used in the introduction.
- Summarize the main points you made in the body of the paper.
- Predict what will happen if the situation continues.
- Suggest a solution to the problem.
- Include a significant quotation.
- Reuse the same technique you used in the introduction. For example, if you described a representative case or scene in the introduction, return to that case or scene.

2. *Working with a small group, complete this composition. Write an introduction in the first row and a conclusion in the last row. Use techniques suggested in this section. You do not need to complete the body of the composition. Share your results with the class.*

Introduction • interest catcher • background information • thesis statement	 Schools should spend more money on female sports than they have in the past.
Body	There are three reasons why girls should have more opportunities to participate in sports.

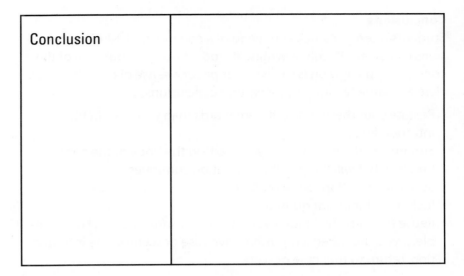

Conclusion	

Writing an Opinion

Write an opinion paper about the value or harm of sports in general or about a particular sport. Be sure to support your opinion with details and examples.

Editing and Rewriting

Editing for Comparatives and Superlatives

When you compare two or more items, it is common to use comparative and superlative forms of adjectives, adverbs, and nouns.

1. *Remember these rules when you are writing comparisons.*

Rules	Examples
Use the comparative form **-er** with one-syllable adjectives or adverbs or with two-syllable adjectives that end in *-y* or *-le*.	This route down the mountain is **simpler.** Some sports are **riskier** than others.

Rules	Examples
Use **more/less** with longer adjectives or adverbs.	Membership is **more expensive** at that gym.
	This trail is **less difficult than** the one we hiked last week.
Use **more/less** with non-count nouns. Use **more/fewer** with count nouns.	That's a **more dangerous** sport.
	We have **fewer players** on our volleyball team this year.
Make sure items in the comparison are in parallel structure.	INCORRECT: Hang gliding is less dangerous than **to swim.**
	CORRECT: Hang gliding is less dangerous than **swimming.**
Use the superlative form **the . . . -est** with one-syllable adjectives or adverbs or with two-syllable adjectives that end in *-y* or *-le*.	That rock was **the steepest.**
	Gabrielle brought **the littlest** kayak I've ever seen.
Use **the most/the least** with longer adjectives or adverbs.	Let's look for **the most strenuous** trails in the area.
Use **the most/the least** with noncount nouns.	This store has **the least expensive equipment** for **the most value.**
Use **the most/the fewest** with count nouns.	We chose the trail with **the fewest streams** to cross.

For more information about comparatives and superlatives, see Reference, page 239.

ANSWER KEY

2. *Correct the errors in comparatives and superlatives in these sentences.*

   a. We went on two climbs. The first one was more easy than the second.

   b. He was the great climber in rock-climbing history.

   c. Rock climbing is most popular than it used to be.

   d. It requires fewest strength than people think.

   e. My mind was more clear after the climb.

   f. That indoor gym has less handholds than needed.

   g. I am more strong now that I climb each weekend.

   h. Is it riskiest than other sports?

   i. It's a more healthy sport than bowling because you are outdoors.

   j. If you climb a lot, your body becomes flexibler.

   k. Golfers get more injuries per year than bowling.

Editing Checklist

Check the Content

1. *Exchange your opinion paper with a classmate. After you read your classmate's paper, answer these questions:*

   ❏ Does the introduction have an interest catcher, enough background information, and a strong statement of opinion?
   ❏ Does the writer support his or her opinion with reasons and specific examples?
   ❏ Does the conclusion make the composition sound complete?

Check the Details

2. *Read your own opinion paper again. If necessary, revise your paper. Add an interest catcher, more details, or a clearer statement of opinion. Then continue checking your paper. Use these questions:*

   ❏ Did you use the correct verb tenses?
   ❏ Are there any passives? Did you use them correctly?
   ❏ Are all the sentences complete?
   ❏ Did you use comparatives or superlatives correctly?

3. *Revise your paper.*

Vocabulary Log

What words or phrases would you like to remember from this chapter? Write five to ten items in your notebook. Examples are on page 12.

Grammar and Punctuation Review

Look over your writing from this chapter. What changes did you need to make in grammar and punctuation? Write them in your notebook.

Review all the grammar and punctuation problems you recorded in your notebook. Make a list of the ones that you still need to work on.

Class Activity **Exercise Cost Analysis**

1 *Make a list of the variety of exercise options in your area. In groups, choose one of the options.*

2 Investigate the facilities, hours, prices, and special features of the option selected.

3 Prepare a cost analysis chart (see pages 181–182) to share with the rest of the class.

Reference

BUSINESS LETTER FORMAT

The format of a business letter is more formal than a personal letter.

This example is the **full block style.** All the lines of text are lined up on the left.

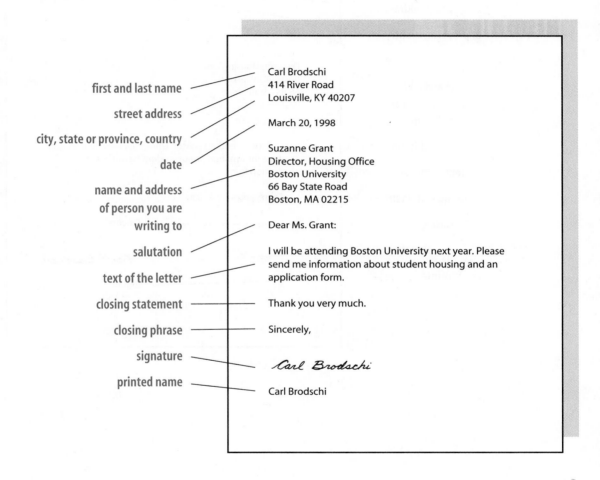

first and last name
street address
city, state or province, country
date
name and address
of person you are
writing to
salutation
text of the letter
closing statement
closing phrase
signature
printed name

Carl Brodschi
414 River Road
Louisville, KY 40207

March 20, 1998

Suzanne Grant
Director, Housing Office
Boston University
66 Bay State Road
Boston, MA 02215

Dear Ms. Grant:

I will be attending Boston University next year. Please send me information about student housing and an application form.

Thank you very much.

Sincerely,

Carl Brodschi

Carl Brodschi

This is the **modified block style.** The first line of each paragraph may be indented five spaces. The address of the sender, the closing phrase, and the signature are all on the right.

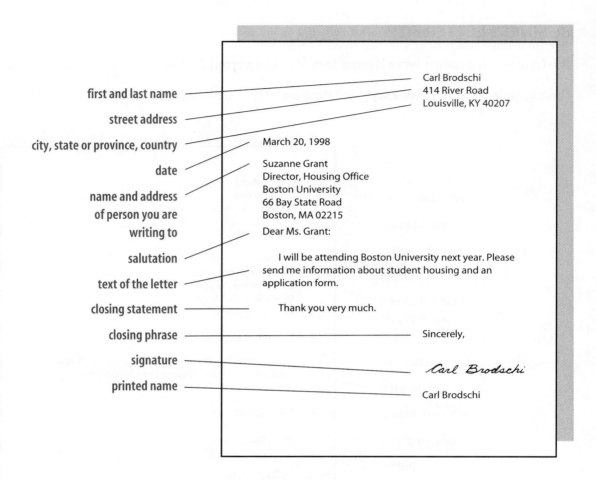

first and last name — Carl Brodschi

street address — 414 River Road

city, state or province, country — Louisville, KY 40207

date — March 20, 1998

name and address of person you are writing to — Suzanne Grant
Director, Housing Office
Boston University
66 Bay State Road
Boston, MA 02215

salutation — Dear Ms. Grant:

text of the letter — I will be attending Boston University next year. Please send me information about student housing and an application form.

closing statement — Thank you very much.

closing phrase — Sincerely,

signature — *Carl Brodschi*

printed name — Carl Brodschi

COMPARATIVES AND SUPERLATIVES

Use these rules to form the comparative and superlative forms of adjectives, adverbs, and nouns.

Rule	Comparative	Superlative	Example
one-syllable adjective or adverb	-er . . . than	the . . . -est	**faster** than (fast) the **hardest** (hard)
two-syllable adjective or adverb ending in **-y;** change the **y** to **i**	-ier . . . than	the . . . -iest	**easier** than (easy) the **busiest** (busy)
two- (or more) syllable adjective or adverb	more . . . than	the most . . .	more **exciting** the most **enthusiastic**
count noun	more . . . than fewer . . . than	the most . . . the fewest . . .	more **jobs** than the most **jobs** fewer **rewards** than the fewest **rewards**
noncount noun	more . . . than less . . . than	the most . . . the least . . .	more **discipline** than the most **discipline** less **money** than the least **money**
irregular forms	**good** **well** **bad** **badly** **far**	**better** **better** **worse** **worse** **farther**	**the best** **the best** **the worst** **the worst** **the farthest**

INFINITIVE AND GERUNDS AS OBJECTS OF VERBS

Rules	Examples
1. Some verbs can only take an infinitive (*to* + verb) object.	I **agreed to do** the work.
2. Some verbs can only take a gerund (verb + *ing*) object.	I don't **mind doing** this kind of work.
3. Some verbs can take either an infinitive or a gerund object.	I **like doing** this kind of work. I **like to do** this kind of project.
4. Some verbs take an infinitive if there is a noun phrase or pronoun object before the infinitive.	He **told me to do** it. She **told the students to do** it.
5. A small number of verbs take an object and a "*to*-less" infinitive.	They **made me do** it. She **let the students do** it.

	infinitive	gerund	either	noun phrase/ pronoun before infinitive	"*to*-less" infinitive		infinitive	gerund	either	noun phrase/ pronoun before infinitive	"*to*-less" infinitive
admit		✔				bother	✔				
advise		✔		✔		care	✔				
(can/can't) afford	✔					cause		✔		✔	
agree	✔					choose	✔			✔	
aim	✔					claim	✔				
allow		✔		✔		coerce	✔			✔	
appear	✔					come	✔				
appoint				✔		complete		✔			
appreciate		✔				consent to		✔			
arrange	✔					consider		✔		✔	
ask	✔			✔		continue			✔		
attempt			✔			control		✔			
avoid		✔				convince				✔	
be	✔					dare	✔			✔	
(can't) bear			✔			decide	✔				
beg	✔			✔		declare				✔	
begin			✔			decline	✔				
believe				✔		decrease		✔			
						defer		✔			

	infinitive	gerund	either	noun phrase/pronoun before infinitive	"to-less" infinitive
defy		✔		✔	
delay		✔			
demand	✔				
deny		✔			
describe		✔			
deserve			✔		
desire	✔				
despise		✔			
determine	✔				
detest		✔			
direct				✔	
discover	✔				
dislike		✔			
dread		✔			
drive				✔	
educate				✔	
empower				✔	
enable				✔	
encourage				✔	
endeavor	✔				
endure		✔			
enjoy		✔			
entitle				✔	
escape		✔			
excuse		✔			
expect	✔		✔		
fail	✔				
favor		✔			
fear		✔			
find				✔	
finish		✔			
forbid				✔	
forget			✔		
get		✔			
give up		✔			
go		✔			
guess				✔	
happen	✔				
hate			✔		
help				✔	✔
hesitate	✔				
hire				✔	
hope	✔				
imagine		✔		✔	
implore				✔	
incite		✔		✔	
increase			✔		
induce				✔	
instruct				✔	
intend	✔			✔	
investigate		✔			
invite				✔	
judge	✔				
keep		✔			
know				✔	
lead				✔	
learn	✔				
let					✔
like			✔		
long	✔				
love			✔		
make					✔
manage	✔				
mean			✔	✔	
mind		✔			
miss		✔			
motivate	✔			✔	
need			✔	✔	
neglect			✔		
notify				✔	
object to		✔			
oblige	✔				
offer	✔				
omit		✔			
order				✔	
permit			✔	✔	
persuade				✔	
plan	✔				
pledge	✔				
postpone		✔			
prefer			✔	✔	
prepare	✔			✔	
pretend	✔				
proceed	✔				

	infinitive	gerund	either	noun phrase/ pronoun before infinitive	"to-less" infinitive
promise	✔			✔	
propose		✔			
prove	✔				
put off		✔			
quit			✔		
recall		✔			
refuse	✔				
regret			✔		
remember			✔	✔	
remind				✔	
report				✔	
request				✔	
require		✔		✔	
resent		✔			
resist		✔			
resolve	✔				
resume		✔			
return	✔			✔	
risk		✔			
rule	✔				
save		✔			
say	✔				
see		✔			✔
seek	✔				
seem	✔				
select				✔	
send				✔	

	infinitive	gerund	either	noun phrase/ pronoun before infinitive	"to-less" infinitive
(can/can't) stand		✔			
start			✔		
state				✔	
stimulate				✔	
stop			✔		
strive	✔				
struggle	✔				
suggest		✔			
suppose	✔				
swear	✔				
teach				✔	
tell				✔	
tempt				✔	
tend	✔				
think				✔	
threaten	✔				
train				✔	
trust				✔	
try			✔		
understand			✔		
undertake	✔				
urge				✔	
wait	✔				
want				✔	
warn				✔	
wish	✔			✔	

IRREGULAR SIMPLE PAST TENSE VERBS

Base	Simple Past	Past Participle	Base	Simple Past	Past Participle
awake	awoke	awoken	leave	left	left
bear	born	born	lend	lent	lent
beat	beat	beaten	let	let	let
become	became	become	lie	lay	lain
begin	began	begun	light	lit/lighted	lit/lighted
bend	bent	bent	lost	lost	lost
bet	bet	bet	make	made	made
bid	bid	bid	mean	meant	meant
bite	bit	bitten	meet	met	met
bleed	bled	bled	prove	proved	proven/proved
blow	blew	blown	put	put	put
break	broke	broken	quit	quit	quit
bring	brought	brought	read	read	read
build	built	built	rid	rid	rid
burn	burnt/burned	burnt/burned	ride	rode	ridden
burst	burst	burst	ring	rang	rung
buy	bought	bought	rise	rose	risen
cast	cast	cast	run	ran	run
catch	caught	caught	say	said	said
choose	chose	chosen	see	saw	seen
come	came	come	seek	sought	sought
cost	cost	cost	sell	sold	sold
creep	crept	crept	send	sent	sent
cut	cut	cut	set	set	set
deal	dealt	dealt	shake	shook	shaken
dig	dug	dug	shine	shone	shone
dive	dove	dived	shoot	shot	shot
	(British: dived)		shrink	shrank	shrunk
do	did	done	shut	shut	shut
draw	drew	drawn	sing	sang	sung
dream	dreamt/dreamed	dreamt/dreamed	sink	sank	sunk
drink	drank	drunk	sit	sat	sat
drive	drove	driven	sleep	slept	slept
eat	ate	eaten	slide	slid	slid
fall	fell	fallen	slit	slit	slit
feed	fed	fed	speak	spoke	spoken
feel	felt	felt	spend	spent	spent
fight	fought	fought	spin	spun	spun
find	found	found	split	split	split
fit	fit	fit	spread	spread	spread
fly	flew	flown	spring	sprang	sprung
forbid	forbid/forbade	forbidden	stand	stood	stood
forget	forgot	forgotten	steal	stole	stolen
forgive	forgave	forgiven	stick	stuck	stuck
freeze	froze	frozen	sting	stung	stung
get	got	gotten	strike	struck	struck
		(British: got)	swear	swore	sworn
give	gave	given	sweep	swept	swept
go	went	gone	swim	swam	swum
grind	ground	ground	swing	swung	swung
grow	grew	grown	take	took	taken
hang	hung	hung	teach	taught	taught
have	had	had	tear	tore	torn
hear	heard	heard	tell	told	told
hide	hid	hidden/hid	think	thought	thought
hit	hit	hit	throw	threw	thrown
hold	held	held	wake	woke	woken
hurt	hurt	hurt	wear	wore	worn
keep	kept	kept	wet	wet	wet
knit	knit	knitted	win	won	won
know	knew	known	wind	wound	wound or winded
lay	laid	laid	withdraw	withdrew	withdrawn
lead	led	led			

NONCOUNT NOUNS

Some nouns do not have a plural form because we cannot count them. We call these *noncount* nouns. Follow these rules when you use a noncount noun.

Rules	Examples
Noncount nouns are singular. If they are the subject of the sentence, the verb must be singular, too.	The **milk is** on the table. His **news is** not good. The **homework was** easy.
Do not use **a** or **an** with a noncount noun.	We need **milk**.
Use a quantity expression to make a noncount noun countable.	Please get **a gallon of milk**. I have **lots of homework** tonight.

Here are some common noncount nouns.

Category	Example
Groups of similar items	art, clothing, equipment, food, fruit, furniture, garbage, grammar, homework, information, luggage, mail, money, music, news, research, slang, traffic, vocabulary, work
Liquids	beer, blood, coffee, cream, gasoline, honey, juice, milk, oil, shampoo, soda, soup, tea, water, wine
Things that can be cut into smaller pieces	bread, butter, cheese, cotton, film, glass, gold, ice, iron, meat, paper, silver, wood
Things that have very small parts	dirt, flour, grass, hair, rice, sand, sugar
Gases	air, fog, pollution, smog, smoke, steam
Ideas that you cannot touch	advice, anger, beauty, communication, education, fun, happiness, health, help, love, luck, peace, sleep, space, time, truth, wealth
Fields of study	business administration, engineering, nursing
Activities	soccer, swimming, tennis, traveling
Diseases and illnesses	cancer, cholera, flu, heart disease, malaria, polio, small-pox, strep throat
Facts or events of nature	darkness, electricity, fire, fog, heat, light, lightning, rain, snow, sunshine, thunder, weather, wind
Languages	Arabic, Chinese, Turkish, Russian

SPELLING RULES FOR ADDING ENDINGS

To apply spelling rules, remember that the vowels in English are **a, e, i, o,** and **u.** The rest of the letters are consonants. When you add endings to nouns or verbs, follow these rules.

Plural Nouns

For most nouns	add **-s**	**book**	**books**
For nouns that end in **s, x, ch**, or **sh**	add **-es**	**box** **wish**	**boxes** **wishes**
For nouns that end in **z**	double the **z** and add **-es**	**quiz**	**quizzes**
For nouns that end in a consonant + **y**	change the **y** to **i** and add **-es**	**delivery**	**deliveries**

Verb Endings

For verbs that end in a consonant + **e**	drop the **e** and add **-ing** or **-ed**	**hope**	**hoping**	**hoped**
For one-syllable verbs that end in one vowel + a consonant	double the consonant and add **-ing** or **-ed**	**stop**	**stopping**	**stopped**
For two-syllable verbs that have the stress on the second syllable and end in a vowel + a consonant	double the consonant and add **-ing** or **-ed**	**omit**	**omitting**	**omitted**
For verbs that end in a consonant + **y**	change the **y** to **i** and add **-ed** or **-es**	**try**	**tried**	**tries**
For verbs that end in **o**, **(t)ch, s, sh, x,** or **z**	add **-es**	**do** **match** **toss** **wish** **fix** **buzz**	**does** **matches** **tosses** **wishes** **fixes** **buzzes**	

TRANSITION EXPRESSIONS

When you combine sentences or ideas, transition expressions help make your ideas clear.

Rules	Examples
Start with two separate ideas or sentences.	I ate breakfast. I went to the store at 10:00.
Combine the ideas with a **preposition.**	I went to the store **after** breakfast.
Combine the ideas with a **subordinate conjunction.**	I went to the store **after** I ate breakfast. I ate breakfast **before** I went to the store.
Combine the ideas with **an adverbial expression.**	I ate breakfast. **After that,** I went to the store. I went to the store. **Before that,** I ate breakfast.

Here are some common transition expressions.

Transition Expressions	Examples
Time in a Sequence	
Prepositions: after, before, until, since, prior to	We waited **until** 3:15. We waited **until** they came.
Subordinate Conjunctions: after, before, until (till), once, ever since	
Adverbial Expressions:	We weren't angry **at first.** **At first,** we weren't angry.
to express time before the present:	
before that, beforehand, formerly, in the past, earlier, (not) long ago, at first	
to express time now:	
at present, presently, at this point/time, nowadays, currently	
to express time after:	
after that, afterward, later, later on, soon after	
to express time in the future:	
in the future	

Transition Expressions	Examples
Listing	
Adverbial Expressions:	
first, in the first place, in the second place, later on, then, subsequently, from then on, following that, after that, next, finally, last	**First,** try to write down the problem. **Then,** telephone the landlord.
including length of time:	**Since then,** we have had no more problems.
before long, immediately, from then on, following that, since then	
Time: Simultaneous	
Preposition: during	They watch TV **during** dinner.
Subordinate Conjunctions: when, as, while, as long as, whenever	They watch TV **when** they eat dinner.
Adverbial Expressions: meanwhile, in the meantime, at the same time, at that time	I waited in line at the ticket counter. **Meanwhile,** my father returned the rental car.
Contrast	
Preposition: unlike, in contrast to	**Unlike** my sister, I like cold weather.
Subordinate Conjunctions: but, while, whereas	I like cold weather, **but** my sister doesn't.
Adverbial Expressions: however, in contrast, on the other hand, by/in comparison, in fact, on the contrary	I like cold weather. My sister, **on the other hand,** hates it.
Contrast: Concession	
Prepositions: despite, in spite of, regardless of	They had the party outside **despite** the weather.
Subordinate Conjunctions: although, though, even though, while, in spite of/regardless of/despite the fact that	They had the party outside **although** it looked like rain.
Adverbial Expressions: even so, just the same, after all, anyhow, anyway, admittedly, regardless	It looked like rain. **Even so,** they had the party outside.
Contrast: Dismissal and Replacement	
Prepositions: instead of, rather than	They ate a snack **instead of** a big dinner.
Adverbial Expressions: either way, in any case/event, at any rate, no matter how/what, instead	**No matter what** they decide, *I* am going to go on that trip.

Transition Expressions	Examples
Cause-Effect, Results, Reasons	
Prepositions: because of, as a result of, due to, owing to, on account of, in view of, since	She was unhappy **because of** her living situation.
Subordinate Conjunctions: because, since, as, now that, in view of/on account of/because of/ due to the fact that	She was unhappy **because** she didn't like her roommates.
Adverbial Expressions: for this reason, because of this, as a result, therefore, so	**Since** her roommates never talked to her, she didn't feel comfortable in her apartment.
	Her roommates almost never spoke. **Because of this,** she was very unhappy in her apartment.
Condition	
Subordinate Conjunctions: if, unless, whether (or not), even if, only if, in case that, provided that, on condition that, supposing that	**If** it rains, we won't go to the beach.
	We'll go to the beach **unless** it rains.
Consequence	
Adverbial Expressions: in that case, if so, then, otherwise, or else, if not, under those circumstances	If you want to come with us, that's fine. **Otherwise,** we'll meet you there.
Examples	
Preposition: such as	I like sports **such as** ice-skating that keep you warm in the winter.
Adverbial Expressions: for example, as an example, for instance, e.g.	Some winter sports are better than others. **For example,** ice-skating keeps you warm and is great exercise.
Conclusion	
Adverbial Expressions: in conclusion, in summary, to summarize, all in all	**All in all,** we had a wonderful time.
Addition	
Preposition: in addition to	On their trip they visited Alaska **in addition to** the Canadian Rockies.
Adverbial Expressions: also, in addition, moreover, likewise, similarly	He didn't want to spend so much time away. **In addition,** it was too expensive.

Answer Key

I What's in a Name?

CHAPTER 1

Reading (pages 2–5)

2. (pages 3–4)
a. the Grand Hotel b. 28 c. Beijing d. 3,100 e. Li, Wang, Zhang, Liu, Chen
f. 87 million g. Smith h. Lab tests get mixed up, love letters get sent to
the wrong person, and people get arrested by mistake.
3. (pages 4–5)
b. are at a very low point. c. by his own counting d. the supply of family
names is decreasing e. a small part of something f. not selecting
unusual names g. what a person is meant to do with his or her life
h. not willing to try new names

Reflect on Reading (page 5)

Names: c Lists: e Dates: b Ages: a

Preparing to Write: Analyzing the Style and Format (pages 5–9)

2 (pages 8–9)
a. letter: used wrong surname; fax: spelling mistake; e-mail message:
sent to the wrong Hillary
b.

	Letter	Fax	E-mail
name and address of sender	✓		
name and address of receiver	✓		
date	✓	✓	✓
salutation with a colon (:)	✓		
a sentence or two of greeting			
the main message in the first couple of sentences	✓	✓	✓
a closing	✓	✓	✓
formal use of language	✓	✓	
informal use of language			✓
incomplete sentences			
indenting the first line of a paragraph			
single spacing in paragraphs	✓	✓	✓
double spacing between paragraphs	✓	✓	✓

c. the use of the salutation with a colon instead of "Hi" or
the person's name by itself; the expression "Thank you (very much)"
instead of "Thanks"; the closings; the complete address of sender and
receiver (letter); complete sentences
d. the e-mail writer seems friendlier because of the use of
"Hi" and "Thanks"

Editing for Sentence Completeness (pages 9–11)

2. (page 11)
a. are different b. me because c. identities. Others . . . OR ; others . . .
d. surnames. Keeping e. are equal. f. names, I . . . confusion because

CHAPTER 2

Reading (pages 14–20)

2. (page 17)
True statements: b, c, d, e, f, h
3. (pages 17–18)

traditional	woman takes husband's last name	Jane Dow → Jane Snow when she marries Joe Snow
nontraditional	woman keeps birth name	*Cathie Whittenburg → Cathie Whittenburg*
	couple merges their last names	Nancy Herman and Don Perlmutter → the Perlmans
	woman keeps birth surname as middle name	*Hillary Rodham → Hillary Rodham Clinton*
	couple hyphenates name	*Jeff Nicholson → Jeff Nicholson-Owens or Dawn Owens → Dawn Owens-Nicholson*
	man takes wife's last name	Joseph Bubeck → Joseph Keel

4. (pages 18–19)
a. Illinois grade school students b. that the male line of heritage is important c. women taking their husband's last name d. if women take
their husband's last name e. women keeping their birth name f. intolerant or traditional g. a cement link between husband and wife h. Illinois Department of Motor Vehicles i. his credit card company; change
his name over the phone j. he liked his wife's last name better than his
k. what last name to give their children
5. (page 20)

describe a person's background	*religious, married, males, political, conservative, with more education and higher income*
categorize groups of people	*couples, students, mothers, professionals, men, women, people with more education and higher income, conservative voters, married women, people who grew up in large cities, siblings, sons, the groom's family, the bride's family, grandkids, children*
are related to types of attitudes	*sexist, non-traditional, traditional, tolerant, conservative, discriminatory, feminist*
are related to reporting research	*conducted studies, surveyed, researching, dissertation*
have meanings similar to these words	a. *a non-issue* b. *heritage* c. *tolerant* d. *the norm* e. *to fight tooth and nails* f. *logistical hassles* g. *discrimination*

CHAPTER 3

Reading 1 (pages 22–27)

2. (page 24)
a. secure a child's future; make a difference in that child's success in the future
b. bring unhappiness in life
c. restrict the naming
d. approved
e. lost

3. (page 25)

Word	Possible Meaning	Strategy (Context, Related Word, Word Root/Affix, Own Knowledge)
a. appropriate	good	(will vary)
b. secure	help make good	
c. strokes	movements with a pen or pencil	
d. upright	straight, tall	
e. feminine	woman-like	
f. strict	direct, definite	
g. genealogy	family tradition	
h. paternal	of the father	
I. indicate	show	
j. Hispanicized	made Hispanic	
k. parental	of parent(s)	
l. intervene	come in the middle of	

4. (page 25)
3, 1, 2

5. (page 26)
a. repeat a family name b. part of the name is the same for one generation c. biblical names d. name chosen for good luck e. boys given the name of the paternal grandfather f. daughter and son of Gudrun g. named after famous people h. name chosen for good luck i. named after a famous person

Reading 2 (pages 27–29)

1. (page 27)
4, 2, 3, 1

2. (page 29)
a. 1 b. 4 c. 1 d. 2

Targeting: Collocations for Describing Names
(pages 29–32)

2. (pages 31–32)
b. think of c. name or call d. calls e. use/call him by f. gave g. changed, from, to h. by i. called

Preparing to Write 2 (pages 33–36)

2. (pages 35–36)
a. 1, 3 b. 1, 3 c. 1 d. 1 e. 2

Editing for Verb Tense Errors (pages 36–39)

2. (page 38)
b. (correct) c. called d. have always loved e. changed f. wanted (or change "expressed" to "expresses") g. gave h. changed i. don't j. will change

3. (pages 38–39)
a. struck b. prevented c. ruled d. was e. affects f. live/have been living g. kept h. was/had been i. was written j. was k. lived

2 Food for Thought

CHAPTER 4

Reading 1 (pages 43–46)

2. (pages 44–45)
a. munchies b. cheer yourself up c. chill out d. snack e. appetite f. sensory g. soaring h. tension i. luscious j. indulging k. down l. yearn m. nutritious n. gender o. soothes p. standpoint q. serotonin and endorphins

3. (pages 45–46)
a. 1 b. 2 c. 2 d. 2 e. 1 f. 3 g. 3

Reading 2 (pages 46–49)

2. (page 48)

meats and meat substitutes	fruits and vegetables
milk and dairy products	grains (breads and cereals)

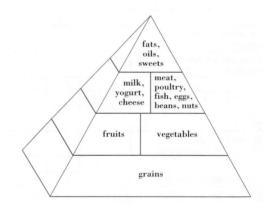

4. (pages 48–49)
a. G, S; b. S, G; c. S, G; d. G, S

5. (page 49)

Verb	Noun	Adjective
improve	improvement	improved
	health	healthy
	deficiency	deficient
diet	diet	dietary
govern	government	
recommend	recommendation	recommended
vary	variety	various
	day	daily
	nutrient	nutritious

Reading 3 *(pages 50–52)*

2. *(pages 51–52)*
a. takes place, gather; b. <u>maple syrup covers fried dough in the shape of a beaver tail/a combination of french fries, brown gravy, and curd cheese</u>; yes; c. bar; d. <u>fried pork cutlets</u>; <u>fried pork skin</u>; <u>a pork broth with a floating hunk of corn on the cob</u>; <u>a stew of cow stomach and chile</u>; e. 3; f. <u>small, light brown, peanut-flavored corn snacks</u>; g. yes; there is a variety of snacks. h. 2

Editing and Rewriting: Editing for Consistency in Charts and Lists *(pages 54–56)*

2. *(page 55)*
b. relax c. repeat d. **Modern Remedy** e. eat some sorbet f. **Day 2** g. cucumbers on your eyelids h. minutes.

CHAPTER 5

Reading *(pages 59–63)*

1. *(page 59)*
[2] Eating Internationally [3] Leaving Food Or Not [4] Serving Something to Drink [5] Keeping Your Hands in the Right Place [6] Using Tableware [8] Cleaning Hands [9] Using a Toothpick [10] Observing Carefully

Targeting: Ways to Give Advice *(pages 64–65)*

2. *(pages 64–65)*
a. should refuse; impolite to ask b. to refuse c. to use d. should put e. wait to see f. to decide g. to fill

Editing and Rewriting: Editing for Gerunds and Infinitives *(pages 67–69)*

2. *(page 68)*
b. to show (I) c. Eating (G) d. Burping (G) e. to burp (I) f. eating (G); to show (I) g. to change (I); to cut (I); to keep (I) h. to keep (I); having (G); hearing (G); keeping (G)
3. *(pages 68–69)*
a. Teaching *(Note: "To teach" is grammatically correct but less common.)* b. to learn c. having d. showing e. to learn f. to understand g. (correct)

CHAPTER 6

Reading 1 *(pages 71–74)*

4. *(page 72)*
[2] doctor at restaurant [3] health benefits on menu [4] delicious food [5] exotic selections
6. *(page 73)*
a. physician b. pharmacist c. chef d. an instant hit e. selections f. exotic
7. *(page 73)*
a. attract attention b. approach to c. medical check-up d. certified e. prescribe f. soothe the nerves g. sound like

Reading 2 *(pages 74–76)*

4. *(page 76)*
<u>food adjectives</u>: *possible answers:* spicy, teriyaki, mushy, barbecued, sweet, sour, large, standard, homestyle, fresh, delicious, home-made, international, French, Chinese, Scottish, Indonesian, varied, good
<u>decor or atmosphere adjectives</u>: *possible answers:* large, dark, plastic, tropical, thatched, long, narrow, clean, bright, limited, interesting, no (atmosphere)
<u>cost adjectives</u>: affordable, reasonable
<u>service adjectives</u>: fast, friendly

Editing and Rewriting: Editing for Colons and Semicolons *(page 80)*

2. *(page 81)* b, d, e, f

3 Musical Notes

CHAPTER 7

Reading 1 *(pages 86–87)*

1. *(page 86)*
Dar Williams: folk; Chansonnier: medieval; Carmen: opera; Tucker Martine: jazz; The Refreshments: rock; Hank Williams et al.: country; Aerosmith: rock; Dance Hall Crashers: rock; The Marriage of Figaro; opera; Diane Schuur; jazz; Baroque orchestra: baroque; Music in the Park: classical
3. *(page 87)*
a. Aerosmith b. Marriage of Figaro is free; Children 17 and under with a paying adult can go to Music in the Park for free c. cost, location, time, phone number, performer and/or performance

Reading 2 *(pages 87–91)*

2. *(page 89)*
a. the students at class at TCU b. Musical Beginnings c. the other premature babies d. group; computer nor piano lessons e. the other two groups (those who took computer lessons plus those who took neither) f. the researchers g. students h. an instrument
3. *(pages 90–91)*

Lorna Zemke	before birth (prenatal)	Opinion
Brigham Young University	premature babies	Research
Journal of *Neurological Research*	preschoolers (given)	Research
(not mentioned)	older children (given)	Research

Targeting: Word Forms *(pages 91–93)*

1. *(pages 91–92)*

Verb	Noun	Adjective
socialize	socialization	*sociable*
verbalize	verbalization	*verbal*
alert	alertness	*alert*
research	researcher	
reason	reasoning/ reason	*reasonable*
	essence	essential
relate	relationship	*related/ relational*
instruct	*instruction*	*instructional*
develop	*development*	developmental
manage	management	*managing/ managed/ manageable*
	music/musician	musical
compose	composer	
enjoy	enjoyment	*enjoyable*
educate	education	*educated*

2. *(page 92)*
verb endings: -ize; -e
noun endings: -ion, -ness, -er, -ment, -ship
adjective endings: -ed, -able, -ing, -al, -ial
3. *(pages 92–93)*
a. sociable; socialize b. reasoning c. related d. essential e. instruction f. develop g. compose h. enjoyable; enjoyed i. educated

CHAPTER 8

Starting Point *(page 96)*

1. From left to right: Russian balalaika, African thumb piano, and maracas.

Reading *(pages 96–99)*

3. *(page 98)*
a. blowpipe b. fingerholes c. chanter d. windbag e. reedpipes f. dronepipe g. thumbscrew h. strings i. neck j. resonating box k. drumsticks l. hollow container m. head of drum
4. *(page 98)*
a. during the Renaissance b. folk music in Europe and military music in Britain c. Scottish bagpipers blow into a tube connected to the bag; French bagpipers move the bellows with their arms to provide air d. The origin is unknown e. the lute f. bluegrass and some forms of country music g. you press the fingers of one hand at different places on the strings along the neck while you strum or pluck the strings over the resonating box h. with the slave trade i. you strike the head of the drum with the palm of the hand or with some kind of stick j. ceremonial or religious role; also used for communication
5. *(pages 98–99)*
a. a musical instrument
b.

	Gives information about the history or typical use	Shows how the instrument works	Shows the materials or structure of the instruments
was common during	✓		
work when air is moved from . . .		✓	
in the old days	✓		
has reed pipes			✓
were made from a whole skin of an animal/with . . .			✓
The origin of the . . .	✓		
. . . instrument with a circular box attached			✓

	Gives information about the history or typical use	Shows how the instrument works	Shows the materials or structure of the instruments
To play the . . . , you press the fingers of one hand at different places on the strings while you . . .		✓	
The . . . developed from the . . .	✓		
drummers strike the . . . with a . . .		✓	
. . . are most often used to . . .	✓		
Historically . . .	✓		

Preparing to Write: Analyzing Parts of Definitions *(pages 100–101)*

1. *(page 100)*

	Term	Category	Difference
a.	electronic music	music	that is generated or reproduced electronically
b.	synthesizer	an electronic musical instrument	that is used to generate or control electronic sounds
c.	clavichord	a string instrument	with keys developed in the fourteenth century
d.	bagpipe drones	pipes	that make a continuous low sound
e.	musette	a French bagpipe	that has bellows instead of an air tube
f.	balalaika	a Russian instrument	with a triangular body that has a flat back and a slightly curved front
g.	dombra	an instrument in the guitar family	that predates the balalaika

2. *(page 101)*
b. A musician is a person who plays music. c. A piano is a keyboard instrument that/which has hammers that strike wire strings. d. A musical arranger is a person who adapts a musical composition to a particular style of performance or instruments. e. Reggae is a type of music that/which has a particular beat that/which originated in Jamaica.

Editing and Rewriting: Editing for Adjective Clauses and *of* and *for* Phrase Errors *(pages 101–103)*

2. *(pages 102–103)*
a. is b. has c. has d. pulling and releasing e. which/that f. leads g. making

CHAPTER 9

Reading 1 (pages 105–109)

1. (page 105)
chronological
4. (page 107)
2. early jazz; 3. standardization of arrangements: 4. bebop style;
5. alternating styles; 6. current jazz
5. (pages 107–108)
a. S, G b. G, S c. S, G d. G, S e. G, S f. S, G g. G, S h. G, S i. S, G
6. (pages 108–109)
a. mixture b. harmonious harmony c. emphasis d. musical e. musicians;
improvise f. arrangement g. traditional h. react i. amplify

Targeting: Transitions (pages 111–114)

2. (page 113)
b. because c. Because of this d. For example e. but
3. (pages 113–114)
a. I like rock music. However, I never go to concerts because they are
too loud.
b. The amplifiers . . . For this reason, doctors . . . c. Because many people . . . , they need hearing aids. d. Doctors recommend . . . For example, they recommend . . . e. . . . peers, so they . . .

Preparing to Write 2: Organizing Support
(pages 115–117)

1. (pages 116–117)
a. time order b. definition, contrast/comparison c. definition, con-
trast/comparison d. definition, cause/effect e. definition,
contrast/comparison f. time order, contrast/comparison, definition

Editing and Rewriting: Editing for Punctuation with Subordinating Conjunctions and Adverbial Expressions (pages 118–119)

2. (page 119)
a, e, f, g

4 The Games We Play

CHAPTER 10

Starting Point (pages 122–123)

1. (pages 122–123)
f. the winner and the loser b. roll the dice c. a deck of cards
a. the person who is "it" d. necessary objects e. playing pieces

Reading (pages 124–125)

2. (page 125)

Description	Examples
What you need	at least 6 children, a yard with hiding places, an empty tin can
How to begin the game	Everyone hides while the person who is "it" hides his or her eyes and counts to 100.
What you say when you see a hidden person	"Over the can for (.......)!"
When the person who is "it" has to begin the game again	When someone kicks the can and frees all the people in jail

Description	Examples
special rules	You can hide only in one yard, the people in "jail" may give clues to hiders about when it is safe to come in and kick the can.
When the game is over	When everyone is in jail

3. (page 125)
c

Preparing to Write 2: Organizing Information
(pages 127–129)

1. (pages 127–129)
b. What You Need c. How to Begin Playing d. The Object of the Game
e. How to Play the Game f. Penalties or Special Rules g. How to Determine the Winner h. Conclusion

Editing for Articles and Nouns in Generalizations
(pages 130–131)

2. (page 131)
a. a game b. a pencil; a small piece c. teams d. a captain (or captains)
e. (correct) f. people g. (correct) h. (correct) i. a slip j. (correct) k. a teammate l. (correct) m. (correct) n. a person; an object o. a player; an action;
a word; a hand OR their hands OR players; actions; gestures; words;
their hands p. teammates q. (correct)

CHAPTER 11

Starting Point (pages 133–134)

1. (page 133)
chess, Monopoly, Clue, Parcheesi

Reading 1 (pages 134–138)

2. (page 136)
b. names of games c. companies that sell games d. things that are
not allowed in games in Austria and Germany e. games that are or
will be on CD-ROM f. what people do in games g. languages that
Scrabble has been published in
3. (page 137)
b. cultural differences c. a language that is complicated to translate
games into d. a game that was not successful everywhere or a game
on CD-ROM e. a successful cross-cultural game or a game on
CD-ROM
4. (pages 137–138)
a. 3 b. 1 c. 2 d. 4 e. 4

Reading 2 (pages 138–141)

2. (pages 140–141)
a. They are viewed as entertainment, acceptable for adults to play.
b. Those that play down the need to win. c. People are not in a serious
state of mind. d. To enjoy yourself. e. They give people a chance to
express their hidden emotions. f. Out of control at work; in control
within the structure of games. g. No.

Targeting: The Language of Summaries
(pages 141–143)

2. (page 143)
a. In; article; "Non-Game Games" b. In their article c. According to
d. also e. give f. claim/state/say g. Furthermore/Moreover/Also/
In addition

Preparing to Write 1: Steps for Writing a Summary
(page 143)

1. *(page 144)*
Games may sell well in one country and be a failure in another.
2. *(page 144)*
b. In their article, "The Games Nations Play," Tate and Croft state that games may sell well in one country and be a failure in another.
3, 4, 5. *(page 144)*
(Answers will vary.)

Editing for Errors with Count Nouns *(pages 146–148)*

2. *(pages 147–148)*
a. games; youngsters b. (correct) c. games d. children e. ideas f. games g. skills h. turns; directions i. expectations; an expectation j. people; skills k. children l. (correct) m. critics n. children; game o. a parent/parents p. a flashlight/flashlights q. (correct) r. relatives

CHAPTER 12

Reading *(pages 151–153)*

1. *(page 151)*
a. 3 b. 4 c. 2 d. 5 e. 1
4. *(page 153)*
a. F b. F c. T d. F e. T f. F g. F h. F

Preparing to Write 1 *(page 153)*

1. *(page 153)*
a. you, it, them, him/her, he/she, their, his/her, your, its
b. you, your
2. *(page 153)*
a. Place . . . and put; Place . . . throw . . . move; place
b. The object of the game is . . . ; The equipment consists of . . . There are Chance and . . . ; Each player is given $1500 . . . ; All remaining . . . ; The player with the highest . . . ; A bankrupt player . . . ; The last player left . . .
c. Each player choose one token . . . while traveling . . . (reduced time clause); After you have completed your play, . . . ; According to the space . . . ; Each time a player's token . . . , whether by . . . ; Whenever you land on . . . ; When you land on property . . . ; When you own all of the properties . . . ; When a player has four houses . . . ; . . . if you owe more . . . ;
d. imperatives: 3, simple sentences: 8, complex sentences with *if* or time clauses 9
e. complex sentences with *if* or time clauses
3. *(page 154)*
a. After you have completed . . . ,
b. headings
4. *(page 154)*
a. is, consists, are, place, put, chooses, is given, go, plays, must keep, throws, starts, place, marked, throw, move, indicated, have completed, passes, reaches, may be entitled, obliged, lands, passes, pays, land, may buy, receive, place, land, owned, collects, printed, own, may buy, erect, has, may buy, erect, are declared, owe, can pay, must . . . retire; left; wins
b. *(present)* is, consists, are, choose, is given, go, plays, throws, starts, passes, reaches, lands, passes, pays, land, receive, land, collects, own, erect, has, erect, owe, wins
(modals in present) must keep, may be entitled . . . obliged (present passive), may buy, may buy, may buy, can pay, must . . . retire
(passive) is given, marked *(reduced)*, indicated *(reduced)*, may be entitled . . . obliged, owned *(reduced)*, printed *(reduced)*, are declared, left *(reduced)*
c. present tense
5. *(page 154)*
a. bold b. no

Editing for Appropriate Tone *(pages 156–157)*

2. *(pages 156–157)*
a. land, lands, draw, throw b. you are, your token c. you are sent

d. your move, your next turn e. delete "but I never sell my card," you roll, your next f. must, have to g. you then, your throw

5 Dates and Mates: Changing Patterns

CHAPTER 13

Reading *(page 162)*

2. *(page 163)*
researcher—*Michael Cunningham*
old theory—men look for *physical attractiveness*
women look for *money/financial resources*
Study 1—# people = *118 women*
Women chose men with more *money and honesty.*
Money not important by itself.
Study 2—# people = *52 men, 54 women, 106 people*

one trait		
women— date or mate	men— for date	men— for mate
good personality (50%)	*physical attractiveness*	*good personality*
physical attractiveness (29%)	*good personality*	*physical attractiveness*
wealth (21%)		

two traits		
women— date or mate	men— for date	men— for mate
good looks plus personality (81%)	*beauty plus personality*	*beauty plus personality*
wealth plus personality (11%)		
good looks plus wealth (8%)		

Study 3—# people = *103 women*
women chose a *high school teacher over a (wealthy, busy) surgeon.*
4. *(page 164)*
money: money, financial resources, wallet, financial status
little money: $20,000, barely scraping by, low financial status
lots of money: rich, big bucks, wealth, $200,000, millionaire
5. *(page 164)*
adjectives: physically attractive, handsome, average looking
nouns: good looks, physical attractiveness, figure, beauty
6. *(page 165)*
a. willingness to listen b. dependability c. a millionaire
7. *(page 165)*
a. the old theory b. experiment c. money d. the teacher e. 103 women f. of the women g. of the women

Targeting: Survey Questions *(pages 166–168)*

3. *(page 168)*
a. 5 b. 6 c. 1 d. 3 e. 7 f. 8 g. 2 h. 4

Editing for Errors in Article Use *(pages 172–173)*

2. *(page 173)*
a. a b. the c. (no article) d. an e. The f. the g. the h. The i. a j. a k. The l. a m. a n. The o. the p. a/the q. the r. the s. the t. a u. (no article) v. the w. a x. a y. the z. the

CHAPTER 14

Reading 1 *(pages 175–178)*

2. *(page 177)*
a. T b. F c. T d. T e. T f. F g. F
4. *(page 177)*
fighting, being patriotic

5. *(pages 177–178)*

Dr. Richard Eisler	professor of psychology	easy way for a man to show he is liberated
Dr. Herb Goldberg	psychologist and author	food and cooking intimate and seductive; way for a man to show he is not macho; man seems safer
Raymond Pellicore	ornamental iron worker	nice to cook and share the responsibilities
Larry Kaplowitz	computer analyst	a lot of women feel intimidated by men who can cook

Reading 2 *(pages 178–181)*

2. *(pages 179–180)*
a. 4 b. 1
3. *(page 180)*
a. 3 b. 1 c. 4 d. 2 e. 5

CHAPTER 15

Reading 1 *(pages 185–187)*

2. *(pages 186–187)*
a. 3; 1; 2 b. 2 c. 2 d. 4
3. *(page 187)*
a. 5 b. 8 c. 6 d. 1 e. 9 f. 10 g. 3 h. 7 i. 4 j. 2

Reading 2 *(pages 187–189)*

2. *(page 189)*
b. Savannah c. St. Paul d. Portland e. St. Paul f. Detroit g. Savannah
h. Detroit i. Savannah

More Editing for Articles *(pages 192–193)*

1. A 2. (no article) 3. a 4. (no article) 5. (no article) 6. a 7. a 8. (no article)
9. (no article) 10. the 11. a/the 12. (no article) 13. (no article) 14. an 15. a
16. a

6 Beyond Your Limits

CHAPTER 16

Starting Point *(pages 196–197)*

1. *(page 196)*
a. rock climbing
b. hang gliding
c. kayaking
d. sky diving
e. bungee jumping

Reading *(pages 197–202)*

2. *(page 199)*

Risky Behavior	Chemical Reactions	Thrill-Seekers
mountain climbing	adrenaline	more focused people

Risky Behavior	Chemical Reactions	Thrill-Seekers
asking for a raise	chemical messenger	usually male
racing fast cars	body chemical	desire for exploration
not wearing a seat belt	dopamine	willing to risk death
sky diving		more easily bored
getting married		extravagant
		excitable
		intensely alive

3. *(pages 199–200)*

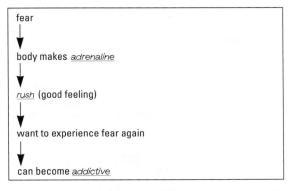

fear
↓
body makes *adrenaline*
↓
rush (good feeling)
↓
want to experience fear again
↓
can become *addictive*

15% of the population have risk-taking gene	
with gene	without gene
respond to *dopamine* are more *extravagant, excitable, and impulsive*	lose *aggressiveness, interest in sex, desire for exploration*

4. *(page 201)*
a. because they want the excitement of thrills b. because they left a secure place to go to an unknown place c. because the chemical messenger dopamine makes people more excitable and impulsive, and therefore willing to take risks d. because young men with higher levels of testosterone take more risks e. they believe women are taught not to take risks, but that this is not a basic physical difference
5. *(page 202)*
a. F b. T c. F d. T e. F f. T g. T h. T

Targeting: Collocations *(pages 202–203)*

2. *(pages 202–203)*

As a verb	As an adjective (including nouns acting as adjectives)
risk death	risky
take risks	risk differences
As a noun	risk-taking differences
risk-taking	
risk takers	
risks	

CHAPTER 17

Starting Point *(pages 204–205)*

3. *(page 205)*
a. 3 b. 4 c. 1 d. 2

Reading *(pages 205–210)*

3. *(page 208)*
b. symptoms c. medical conditions d. environmental changes e. ways to adapt to higher altitudes f. compensatory mechanisms
4. *(page 208)*
slight mild moderate frequent severe acute
5. *(pages 208–209)*
a. at about 18,000 feet b. about 8,000 feet c. brain and lungs d. Acute Mountain Sickness e. mild, moderate, and severe f. mild headache and slight nausea g. severe headaches and frequent vomiting/moderate tiredness h. changes in consciousness, ataxic behavior, severe tiredness, cough, blue or pale color, weakness
6. *(page 209)*

Level of AMS	Treatment
mild	• mild pain relievers (aspirin, ibuprofen, Tylenol) • avoid sedatives (alcohol, narcotic drugs) • rest at present altitude until body adapts
moderate	• pain medication, rest, avoidance of sedatives • careful observation and emergency descent if necessary • supplemental oxygen and steroids
severe	• all of the above with immediate descent

7. *(page 210)*

Term	Context Clue	Definition
slight	with	little or no
acute	or	severe
ataxic	parentheses	unable to walk straight
cyanotic	parentheses	blue or pale
hypoglycemia	parentheses	low blood sugar
sedatives	like	alcohol or narcotic drugs
aspirin, ibuprofen, or Tylenol	such as	(mild) pain relievers

Targeting: Prefixes and Roots *(pages 210–212)*

1. *(pages 210–211)*
a. again or back b. down or away from c. too much d. not e. above; below
2. *(page 212)*
a. biological b. water c. push

Preparing to Write 1: Understanding the Question *(pages 212–213)*

1. *(pages 212–213)*
b. D c. C–R d. C–C e. CL f. D g. C–C h. C–R i. EX j. C–R k. D l. C–R m. CL n. C–C o. D p. C–R q. C–R r. P s. C–C t. C–R u. EX v. C–C w. P x. CL y. C–C z. EX aa. C–R bb. D

Preparing to Write 2: Organizing Your Response *(pages 213–214)*

1. *(page 214)*
b. There are several differences between Mild AMS and Severe AMS. c. The three types of Acute Mountain Sickness are . . . d. Acute Mountain Sickness means . . . e. Climbers can take several steps to avoid getting AMS.

Editing for Use of Active or Passive Voice *(pages 215–217)*

2. *(pages 216–217)*
b. push c. are lost; exercise; overexert d. (no errors) e. have not taken in f. (no errors) g. may have declined h. (no errors) i. (no errors) j. should be taken in; should be drunk k. (no error) l. is enhanced/will be enhanced m. is delayed n. may experience o. can be made p. (no errors) q. is dissolved; should be added r. (no error)

CHAPTER 18

Starting Point *(pages 219–221)*

1. *(pages 219–220)*
a. 3 b. 2 c. 1

Reading 1 *(pages 221–225)*

2. *(page 224)*
a. F b. F c. T d. F e. F f. T g. F h. F i. T j. T
3. *(pages 224–225)*
a. participants b. drowning c. the bends d. verify e. ankle f. fracture g. frostbite h. lacerations i. avalanche j. scrape k. sprain l. tendinitis m. bruises

Reading 2 *(pages 225–227)*

2. *(page 227)*
b. athletes c. greater chance of unwanted pregnancy d. cholesterol e. suffering
3. *(page 227)*

Study (year)	Results
N.C.A.A. News, June 1995	black female college athletes — graduation rate 58% compared with 41%
Ms. Foundation (1991)	female athletes — depression less likely
National Cancer Institute (1994)	reduce risk of breast cancer
government research (1997)	• team — positive effect — growth and development • better grades, less likely to drop out, more likely to go to college • less stress • less likely to be depressed • fewer health problems, better social skills, more self-confident, healthier self-images, less likely to have an unwanted pregnancy • Poor girls missing out on opportunities. • Still discrimination against girls as athletes.

Preparing to Write 2: Writing Introductions and Conclusions *(pages 229–232)*

1. *(pages 229–230)*
a. <u>According to Benita Fitzgerald Mosley, Olympic gold medalist and director of the U.S. Olympic Training Center, if you participate in sports, you gain a base of strength that stays with you throughout your life.</u> b. surprising fact; <u>Recent studies show that girls who begin sports at an early age are less likely to have teenage pregnancies than girls who do not participate in sports.</u> c. description of a scene; <u>But most of all, you know you have what it takes to get to the top.</u>

d. question; <u>Climbing is [addictive], according to Jim Wickwire, world-class mountain climber.</u> e. relevant quotation; <u>If you really want to succeed in life, you have to play as hard as you work.</u>

Editing for Comparatives and Superlatives *(pages 232–234)*

2. *(page 234)*
a. easier b. the greatest climber c. more popular d. less strength e. clearer f. fewer handholds g. stronger h. riskier i. healthier j. more flexible k. bowlers

Text Credits

Pages 151–152: Monopoly®, the distinctive design of the game board, the four corner squares, as well as each of the distinctive elements of the board and the playing pieces are trademarks of Hasbro, Inc. for its property trading game and game equipment. ©1998/1999 Hasbro, Inc. All rights reserved. Used with permission.

Page 162: Adapted from Malcolm Ritter, "Money can't buy love, they say" as it appeared in the *Seattle Post-Intelligencer*, August 12, 1996. Copyright © 1996 by the Associated Press. Reprinted by permission of the Associated Press.

Page 176: Copyright © 1990 by the New York Times Company. Reprinted by permission.

Page 179: Copyright © 1992, the *Washington Post*. Reprinted with permission.

Page 180: Pam Gregory-Jones, "Lunch among the lupines" from the *Seattle Times*, February 12, 1997. Copyright ©1997 The Seattle Times Company. Reprinted by permission of the *Seattle Times* and Pam Gregory-Jones.

Pages 185–186: Adapted from "Love Through the Ages" by Denise Hamilton from the *Los Angeles Times*, January 9, 1995.

Pages 192–193: "Long-Lost Lovers" adapted from "Old Flames Burn Hottest, Says Study of Long-Lost Lovers" from the *Seattle Times*, 1994.

Page 198: Adapted from "Are you a risk taker?" from *Behavioral Expressions and Biosocial Bases of Sensation Seeking* by Martin Zuckerman. Copyright © 1994. Reprinted with the permission of Cambridge University Press.

Pages 198–199: Adapted text from "The Risk Takers" by Carol Ostrom, the *Seattle Times, Pacific Magazine*, October 20, 1996.

Pages 206–207: Adapted from *The Outward Bound Wilderness First-Aid Handbook* by Jeff Isaac and Peter Goth. Copyright © 1991 by Lyons & Burford Publishers. Reprinted by permission of The Lyons Press.

Pages 216–217: Adapted text from "Walking, running, and playing in summer heat: the risk of dehydration often goes unrecognized" by Jane E. Brody, the *New York Times*, June 12, 1996.

Pages 222–223: Copyright © 1995 by the New York Times Company. Reprinted by permission.

Photo Credits

Page 1: © John Coletti/The Picture Cube, Inc.   Page 15: (top, left) © Jeffrey W. Myers/Stock Boston; (bottom, right) © James Carroll/Stock Boston.   Page 41: (left) © Chuck Wyrostok/Appalight; (right) © Frank Ward.   Page 70: (top, left) © Frank Ward; (bottom, right) © Frank Ward.   Page 71: AP/Wide World Photos.   Page 84: (left) © Michael Grecco/Stock Boston; (right) © David Corio/Retna, Ltd.   Page 85: (top, left) © Andrea Burns; (top, right) © David Corio/Retna, Ltd.; (bottom, left) © Michael Grecco/Stock Boston; (bottom, center) © David Corio/Retna Ltd.; (bottom, right) © Michael K. Daly/The Stock Market.   Page 96: (left) © Robert Ullmann/Design Conceptions; (center) © Chuck Wyrostok/Appalight; (right) © Robert Ullmann/ Design Conceptions.   Page 104: (left) © David Redfern/Redferns/Retna, Ltd.; (center) © David Redfern/Redferns/Retna, Ltd.; (right) © Max Jones files/Redferns/ Retna, Ltd. Page 111: Erica Echenberg, © Redferns/Retna, Ltd.   Page 121: © Jean-Claude LeJeune.   Page 159: (left) © Michael McGovern/The Picture Cube, Inc.; (right) © Frank Ward.   Page 184: (left) © Joel Gordon; (center) © Joel Gordon; (right) © Spencer Grant/The Picture Cube, Inc.   Page 195: (left) © Michael A. Dwyer/Stock Boston; (right) © Fredrik D. Bodin/Stock Boston.   Page 196: (top, left) © Michael A. Dwyer/Stock Boston; (top, right) © Fredrik D. Bodin/Stock Boston; (bottom, left) © Kirk R. Williamson/The Picture Cube, Inc.; (bottom, center) © Bob Kramer/Stock Boston; (bottom, right) © Frederick McKinney/FPG International.